*Edinburgh Military*

# Tattoo

Roddy Martine lives in Edinburgh and has written over twenty books on Scottish interest subjects ranging from *Scottish Clan and Family Names – Arms, Origins and Tartans; Scotland – The Land and the Whisky* to *Time Exposure: The Life of Brodrick Haldane*, photographer. He is co-author of the bestselling *Living in Scotland* and *Living in the Highlands*. He is a contributing editor to *Caledonia* magazine, writes for a wide range of UK newspapers and periodicals, and is a regular radio and television broadcaster on social and current affairs topics.

D1513643

# Edinburgh Military Tattoo

## Roddy Martine

ROBERT HALE · LONDON

© *Edinburgh Military Tattoo Ltd 2001*
*First published in Great Britain 2001*

ISBN 0 7090 6919 7

Robert Hale Limited
Clerkenwell House
Clerkenwell Green
London EC1R 0HT

2 4 6 8 10 9 7 5 3 1

The right of Roddy Martine to be identified as
author of this work has been asserted by him
in accordance with the Copyright, Designs and
Patents Act 1988.

*A catalogue record for this book is available from the British Library*

Set in 11/16 Sabon by
Derek Doyle & Associates, Liverpool.
Printed by Kyodo, Singapore

# Contents

For Lieutenant-Colonel Leslie Dow, OBE who had always intended that a definitive history of the Edinburgh Military Tattoo should be written, and whose preliminary research made it possible.

# Acknowledgements

It was with considerable foresight that in 1991, Lieutenant Colonel Leslie Dow took the important initiative to circulate the many individuals who had been intimately involved with the Edinburgh Military Tattoo since its earliest beginnings, and who were still living, with a view to writing a history. Following his death in 1991, Major Brian Leishman took on this mantle.

The author therefore wishes to thank the following for their invaluable input: Yvonne Ashby, Brigadier Jock Balharrie, Brenda Banks, Christine Barton, David Ben-Aryeah, Mary Boag, Colonel Ian Cameron, Pixie Campbell, WOI (RSM) Dave Chapman, Ian Christie, Major Robin Cole, Brigadier Frank Coutts, Major Mike Cran, Iain Crawford, Thomas K. Currie, Georg Czerner, Gordon Dean, Alan Dippie, Cath Donaldson, Lord Douglas of Selkirk, Joan and Holly Dow, John and Susan Dymock, *Edinburgh Evening News*, Nils Egelien, Alex Elrick, Clive Fairweather, William Fraser, Phillip Gilmore, General Sir Michael Gow, Major Campbell Graham, Brigadier Bruce Hamilton, Barbara Harper-Nelson, Theresa Holt-Wilson, Alasdair Hutton, Brigadier Melville S. Jameson, Major Peter Johnson, Ian McBain, Stuart McBain, Brigadier David McQueen, Ernie Marchant, Peter and Theave Mitchell, Lieutenant Colonel David Murray, Ian Nimmo, Bruce Niven, Michael Parker, WO1(RSM) Jim Paton, Roy Pratt, Patrick and Hope Ramsay, Brigadier Iain Reid, Iris Ritchie, Alan Roberts, the *Scotsman*, Lieutenant General Sir David Scott-Barrett, Dr Michael Shea, James Lawson Sibbald, Aubrey Singer, Alan W. Smith, Lieutenant Col Bobby Smith, Douglas Smith, Brigadier Nigel Stisted,

Major Gavin Stoddart, Dr Cecil H. Stout, Forbes Taylor, Brigadier Bob Tweedy, Don and Robby Vanderpool, Bob Virtue, Stanley Walker, Colonel Robert Watson, Major John White, Lieutenant General Sir David Young.

## Director's Acknowledgements

The Edinburgh Military Tattoo wishes to acknowledge with gratitude the support given to the Tattoo over fifty years:

Ministry of Defence
City of Edinburgh Council
HQ 2nd Division/The Army in Scotland
HQ 52 Lowland Brigade
Historic Scotland
Lothian and Borders Police
Lothian and Borders Fire Brigade
Scottish Ambulance Service
St Andrew's Ambulance Association
The Scout Association, Edinburgh District
Stewards and voluntary staff

The Tattoo also wishes to thank all those in the business community who have so generously contributed to the event. Our principal supporters are:

Bank of Scotland
Norwich Union
Standard Life
British Gas
British Airways
NAAFI
Pol Roger Champagne
A. F. Noble & Son

# Foreword

BUCKINGHAM PALACE

The Edinburgh Military Tattoo has impressed and entertained audiences for over half a century and in the unique setting of the esplanade of Edinburgh Castle it ranks as one of the most colourful out-of-doors spectacles anywhere in the world. No wonder it continues to play to capacity audiences, and that its reputation has circumnavigated the world.

As a spectator, it is often not at all obvious just how much work goes on behind the scenes to make things happen. However, success stories are created by people, and this book is the roll call of personalities; the producers, the performers, the technicians and the box office staff, all of whom have contributed in some way or another towards making this great event so memorable for successive generations.

We are taken back to the beginning of the Tattoo as a small military parade in Princes Street Gardens, attached to the recently launched Edinburgh Festival. For over five decades it has been a showcase for the best of British and international military prowess. For many of us, the music of the Massed Pipes and Drums of the Scottish Regiments, together with the Massed Bands, played against the dramatic backdrop of the old castle walls, is an unforgettable experience. The lone piper on the castle battlements is a haunting image that touches even the strongest heart.

Every year the Edinburgh Tattoo is seen by over 200,000 people and the world-wide television audience is estimated at 100 million. A remarkable achievement for an event that started 50 years ago with a few rows of chairs for spectators and a demonstration of piping and dancing.

*Anne*

# Illustration Credits

# Introduction

Edinburgh Castle has been a part of me almost throughout my long life. As a boy I relished reading about its history, the people who lived there, the excitements that surrounded it, and the soldiers garrisoned there. I thrilled at the discovery of the Honours of Scotland, and checked my first watch by the boom of the one o'clock gun. I clearly recall walking down Princes Street and, looking up, thinking 'What a Swell lives up there!', little knowing that one day I would be that Swell, the Governor.

And the Tattoo, later, became part of my life: I knew Colonel George Malcolm of Poltalloch, and even better Brigadier Alasdair Maclean of Pennycross – Producers and Directors. Brigadier Jack Sanderson, their successor, had been my commanding officer, and Lieutenant Colonel David Murray, master of the bagpipes and well-known commentator, had been a fellow student with me at Army Staff College. Lieutenant Colonel Leslie Dow, the last Commanding Officer of The Cameronians (Scottish Rifles), who became Producer when the Governor of the day was an ardent and active Tattoo supporter.

Leslie was a personal friend. It was to him, on his retirement, that I suggested a history of this great event should be written. Under Major Michael Parker and now Brigadier Melville Jameson, each adding their own flair and production expertise, what had started with humble beginnings fifty years ago, is now a world famous event, watched by millions across the world on TV screens.

But to capture the unique atmosphere you must be there on the Castle Esplanade, and it was my privilege to take the salute for many years as Governor, and as President of the Royal British Legion Scotland, and equally an honour for my Regiment, The Scots Guards, with whom I served for forty-four years, frequently to take part.

The story of what is now an International Tattoo is told by Roddy Martine in this book, full of detail about personalities, participants, programmes – and problems! International though it may be, it is essentially Scottish, continually adding to the on-going history of our ancient Castle and homeland.

General Sir Michael Gow, GCB

# 1  A Noble Vision

AT least some of Edinburgh's city fathers must have suspected what they were letting themselves in for when in 1945 they gave the city's Lord Provost, Sir John Falconer, the go-ahead for his noble vision, to create in the summer of 1947 a world-focused festival of music and drama. This it was envisaged would be a way in which Scotland's capital could make a contribution towards healing the wounds of a rapacious war which had left most of mankind exhausted and disillusioned.

Remember that here was a city situated on the north-east coast of an island off the north-west coastline of a devastated European continent. Consider what Scotland, indeed Britain, was like in those days, slowly re-adjusting to peace and in the process of rebuilding itself. Then try to grasp what a courageous act it must have been to launch an arts festival at that time, especially for a city not exactly noted for artistic licence.

Post-war austerity meant rationing of almost everything, with that curious tinned meat called spam the staple diet. A Labour Government under Clement Attlee was in power, embarking upon an extensive programme to nationalise industry and reform society. Only shapeless utility garments sold in the clothes shops.

Yet a general sense of deliverance prevailed. In Scotland, enhanced by a Presbyterian psyche, such factors combined to produce a prevailing missionary zeal.

Edinburgh had come through the war virtually unscathed. While Clydeside in the West of Scotland had met the full force of German air aggression, and the far side of the Firth of Forth had taken a pounding from the Luftwaffe, in the capital only one bomb had fallen into Princes Street Gardens. The dour old northern capital remained intact, its monuments and buildings blackened not by war but by the coal fires of a pre-smokeless zone century.

How then would it be possible, or appropriate, for Scotland's capital to give thanks for its salvation?

Rudolph Bing, an Austrian, had come to Britain in 1934 from the Charlottenberg Opera in Berlin and been appointed General Manager of the Glyndebourne Opera. For years he had harboured an ambition to create an arts festival of international renown, but the location where this could take place had remained the problem. Post war, he had already made approaches to Oxford and Cambridge, but inexplicably both of these university towns turned him down.

Then a chance meeting with the artist, author and editor Harvey Wood, at the time Scottish representative of the British Council in Edinburgh, led to an introduction to Sir John Falconer, Lord Provost of Edinburgh. The two men instantly found common ground, albeit coming from very different directions.

Sir John, Bing was later to write, 'was not too well informed of the things I was talking about; Bruno Walter and the Vienna Philharmonic Orchestra were not familiar names to him, but he did immediately recognise that here was an idea that might have cultural importance for the British Isles and economic significance for Edinburgh.'

The economic significance for Edinburgh was the driving force. Next an approach was made to the fledgling Arts Council of Great Britain, and at a meeting of the Corporation of the City of Edinburgh on 26 September 1946, much to everybody's amazement, the finance necessary to seed the project was volunteered.

From that moment on the miracle unfolded, and the following year, on Sunday 24 August 1947, the Edinburgh Festival of Music and Drama, as it was then called, was born with a concert in Edinburgh's Usher Hall attended by HM Queen Elizabeth and the 17-year-old Princess Margaret.

In the three warm, sunny weeks of that August of 1947, the old city revelled in its new found cosmopolitan celebrity. Famous names such as John Barbirolli, Kathleen Ferrier, Peter Pears, Elizabeth Schumann and Malcolm Sargent all featured. Bernard Miles, Trevor Howard and Patricia Burke appeared in *The Taming of the Shrew*; Alec Guinness starred in Ralph Richardson's production of *Richard II*, and the ballerina Margot Fonteyn danced in *The Sleeping Beauty* at the Empire Theatre.

Dr Cecil H. Stout, who two decades later was to become City Chamberlain and Director of Finance, recalled that in order to give further impetus to what was happening throughout the city it was decided, following a series of informal conversations between Lord Provost Falconer and Sir Philip Christison, General Officer Commanding the Army in Scotland, that a military spectacle of some kind would be a welcome addition to the programme. Naturally the Army, with a view to recruitment, were only too happy to oblige.

To begin with standing room and a few rows of chairs were provided for a demonstration of piping and dancing on the Esplanade. Dr Stout recalled, 'We (the City Chamberlain's Office) were involved as I remember going to the Esplanade one wet evening to find the Queen of the Netherlands sitting on a chair with her umbrella up cheerfully enjoying the performance.'

The following year the military bands of the 1st Royal Scots and 1st Cameronians played in Princes Street Gardens and on the Castle Esplanade on alternate evenings. There were displays of drill, Highland dancing and a thirty-twosome reel was danced. On one occasion, one of the Highland dancers from the Royal Scots danced himself off the platform raised several feet above the ground. He was unhurt, but was banished the next day to join the 2nd Battalion stationed in Trieste.

1.1 (*overleaf*) Beating Retreat on the Castle Esplanade, from a painting by Christopher Clark RI (1875–1942)

In 1949, the first formal link between Edinburgh Corporation and Scottish Command took place with two military displays, one in the Ross Bandstand in Princes Street Gardens, the second at the Castle. The man chosen to produce these was Lieutenant Colonel George Malcolm of Poltalloch, fresh from the triumph of orchestrating a widely applauded military display at the Kelvin Hall in Glasgow.

Based on a popular pre-World War Two song played at the last Aldershot Tattoos, the first of these performances was called *Something about a Soldier* and featured music by the Royal Scots and Highland Light Infantry (The City of Glasgow Regiment). Community singing at the beginning of each performance was conducted by W. Elliot Dobie, and there were displays of 'precision' and 'agility' from The Royal Scots, and demonstrations of Scottish dancing from the Women's Royal Army Corps.

A report in the *Scotsman* newspaper provided a contemporary response:

> Before ten o'clock Mr W. Elliot Dobie led the huge crowd in community singing, and many men and women were visibly moved when, towards the end of the programme, he asked them to join in the song so closely associated with the great Scottish comedian who was lying gravely ill: *Keep right on to the end of the Road*. The crowd took it up, thousands of voices joining in the words which took on a deeper meaning than ever before.

The great Scottish comedian was, of course, Sir Harry Lauder, who died not long afterwards.

In the same year, George Malcolm produced *The King's Men*, a display at the castle which included a Changing of the Guard by The 9th Lancers and The Scots Guards, as well as a selection of musical items. Again, it was much applauded. The audience for that first Castle spectacle was limited to 2,500, all standing, but the potential for ongoing spectacles in such a fine setting was established.

Fig 1.2

**EDINBURGH FESTIVAL 1949**

*Souvenir Programme*

**AT THE CASTLE**
SCOTTISH COMMAND
*presents*

**"THE KING'S MEN"**
A MILITARY DISPLAY
*produced by*
LIEUT.-COLONEL G. I. MALCOLM OF POLTALLOCH

*Music by the Bands of*
THE ROYAL SCOTS *(The Royal Regiment)*
*and*
THE HIGHLAND LIGHT INFANTRY
*(The City of Glasgow Regiment)*

And it was then that Sir Andrew Murray, who had succeeded Sir John Falconer as Lord Provost, began the arrangement, subsequently endorsed by his successors, of inviting the General Officer Commanding the Army in Scotland to present a military 'show' to be called the Edinburgh Tattoo. Informally it was agreed between them that this would take place annually during the Edinburgh Festival with the hope that a financial contribution might be made to the Festival Society.

If only these two men could have survived to know the full measure of what a partnership this would grow into over the half-century that followed.

Lieutenant-Colonel David Murray, assistant producer from 1975 until 1980, was involved in various aspects of the Tattoo from the very beginning, and gave the following account of how the name 'Tattoo' came to be adopted for military musical spectacles.

A Tattoo is the traditional signal, given originally by drum beat, and latterly by bugle or trumpet call, which warned British soldiers to return to their quarters for the night. During the 1st Duke of Marlborough's triumphant wars in the Low Countries in the early days of the eighteenth century, Dutch innkeepers turned off the liquor taps – 'Tap-toe' – and the drums continued to beat for half an hour, the period of grace during which the soldiers were allowed to make their way home. The custom eventually developed into a ceremonial performance of military music by massed bands a few hours after sunset.

The tradition of including a hymn in the closing stages of the ceremony derives from a custom of the Imperial Army of Czarist Russia in which their soldiers, conscripted virtually for life from the pious peasant masses, sang a chorale after the Tattoo had been sounded. The custom spread to the Catholic armies of Austria and to the predominantly Lutheran Army of Prussia, where the Tattoo ceremony was developed into an impressive torchlight parade.

During the latter half of the nineteenth century, performances by massed regimental bands became popular in the largest garrison towns in Britain, and these, following the Continental practice, came to include an evening hymn, often *Abide with Me*. Certain of the old Regiments of the British Army, such as the 10th Hussars, 12th Lancers, and The Royal Scots Fusiliers maintained the tradition independently by playing a hymn on Sunday evenings between the two calls which marked the beginning and the end of the Tattoo period.

The calls become known as First and Last Post respectively, and were sounded at 9.30p.m. and 10.00p.m. The Hussars, however, began sounding the Last Post at 9.40p.m., the exact time of the death of the Earl of Cardigan who commanded the Regiment between the years 1837 until 1847, while The Life Guards sounded the calls outside barracks gates at the specified original times to commemorate their original function of recalling the soldiers to the barracks.

Such Tattoo rituals have regularly been observed in the British Army and have only recently fallen into abeyance. However, it was at Aldershot, Britain's largest military station, that the scope of these ceremonies was extended to include the wide variety of displays with which the name is now associated, but which has no connection, apart from the music of the bands, with its traditional function.

With the creation in 1922 of the Aldershot Tattoo, held at Britain's largest military station, the word Tattoo became more directly associated with an extravaganza of military might and music for the purpose of entertainment and the demonstration of martial skills.

The agreed basis of the Edinburgh Tattoo was therefore that the army in Scotland would arrange and produce such a performance,

1.3 a & b The 1949 Military Display

while the City Council's departments would make all the administrative arrangements.

Having masterminded the previous 'entertainments,' it seemed only natural, and entirely appropriate, that George Malcolm should be asked to mastermind the transition onto the big stage, and in the second week of August 1950, the first full scale Edinburgh Military Tattoo took place before an audience of 6,000 on the Esplanade of Edinburgh Castle.

# 2   Something About a Soldier

AS the 18th Laird of Poltalloch in Argyll, and hereditary Chief of Clan Malcolm, George Malcolm was descended from one of Scotland's most distinguished West Coast families. His father, Sir Ian Zachary Malcolm, KCMG, was a landowner, diplomat, and member of parliament first for Suffolk (Stowmarket Division), then Croydon. His mother was the daughter of Lillie Langtry, the celebrated Edwardian actress and favourite of Edward VII, and his sister Mary was among the first of the early television broadcasters. An element of show business was therefore in his blood.

George was born in 1903, and following school at Eton, enrolled at Sandhurst where he soon won prominence at boxing. At Sandhurst, his nimbleness of foot also made him an excellent Highland dancer and, according to contemporary accounts, he and Alasdair Maclean of The Queen's Own Cameron Highlanders, who was to join him as Director of the Tattoo in 1950, were considered to be the only officers up to professional dancing standard during the 1930s. Remember that within the Scottish Regiments, proficiency in Highland Dancing was considered an enviable skill for its manly and physical attributes.

George Malcolm had taken part in organising the Aldershot Tattoo of 1938, when his creative input was much admired. With the outbreak of War in Europe, he saw action with the Argyll and Sutherland Highlanders in Palestine (where he was mentioned in Despatches), followed by Egypt, Cyprus, Abyssinia, Malta, and the Pacific. The war ended, and by 1949, it is most likely that he was simply considered the best qualified, possibly the only person capa-

2.1 Lieutenant Colonel George Malcolm of Poltalloch

ble of launching a three-week military Tattoo on the scale envisaged for Edinburgh.

After a war spent as a Staff Officer, he had become a first rate administrator, as was proven when he later commanded The 8th Battalion, The Argyll and Sutherland Highlanders. But it was George Malcolm's sense of Scottish history, enhanced by a life-long involvement with amateur theatricals, writing and directing them rather than acting in them, which gave him the inspiration and incentive to look in other directions. The creation from scratch of a Military Tattoo on the Esplanade of Edinburgh Castle must have seemed at the time the fulfillment of a dream.

So, with George Malcolm as Producer and Lieutenant Colonel Alasdair Maclean from Scotttish Command appointed Director, the first Edinburgh Tattoo was born. It certainly made a lasting impact on the sixteen-year old Robin Malcolm, later to follow in his father's footsteps by enlisting in the Argyll and Sutherland Highlanders.

'My parents had divorced, and my sister and I were wards of the Chancery Court with holidays mathematically split between our mother and father,' he recalled. 'The way dates worked out, 1950 was the only year our time in Scotland coincided with the Tattoo, which we watched from the dark recess of the VIP Box. Our highlight was meeting Mary Martin, the star of the film *South Pacific*.'

Robin spent two days seconded to help Mike Todd, the film producer, fourth husband of Hollywood star Elizabeth Taylor. Todd was making a documentary film on the Tattoo by daylight one day, and the Highland Games at Murrayfield on the following. It was Robin's first lesson in diplomacy.

'He wore a tartan shirt, had a commanding voice, and smoked a large cigar,' was Robin's memory of the man who went on to produce the film *Around the World in 80 Days*, based on Jules Verne's novel about an around the world balloon trip, and who eight years later was to be killed in an air crash. 'He was very demanding, and my job was to shield majors and above from him. I learnt a lot about public relations as a result.'

*[handwritten margin note: WEATHER establishes precedent for future.]*

romotional expectations attached to Todd's subse-
remature. The following year, Philip Gilmore, an
who served with the RASC for twenty-one years
y with Alasdair Maclean, found himself posted to
w that the film was showing in a local cinema.
followed one about The Vienna Boys' Choir,' he
the Gathering of the Clans and there was no
a Tattoo at all!'
attendance in excess of 100,000, despite the
the Edinburgh Tattoo of 1950 established the
precedent for the future. It proved that an out-of doors, all-weather
spectacular in Scotland could work, and more to the point, that
people of all generations would pay to come and see it. Philip
Gilmore remembers one particularly soaking night when Colonel
Maclean instructed the performers to give a round of applause to the
audience for their stamina in sitting through the entire performance.

Eighteen normal evening shows were given that year, one on
Saturday afternoon, primarily for a young audience; and so that
artistes taking part in other Festival activities would have an opportunity to attend, a special midnight performance also took place.

Then there was an incident. During a Thursday performance one
of the participants took a tumble, and the cause was immediately
apparent. All soldiers taking part in the Tattoo were paid one shilling
and six pence (7½p) each per performance; sergeants, three shillings
and six pence (17½p), and Thursday was their pay day. To celebrate,
the men would promptly set off for the nearest Royal Mile pub,
usually the Ensign Ewart or Deacon Brodie, where visiting tourists
were often only too happy to buy a round for the heroes of the
Tattoo.

The way in which Scottish Command responded to the situation is
only to be admired. There was no curtailment imposed on the freedom of the soldiers off-duty, but in order to avoid a recurrence of the
'incident', it was agreed that in future there would be no Thursday
Tattoo performance.

And times were changing. After four successful years, it was universally accepted that the large scale Edinburgh Festival of Music and Drama had arrived at a cross-roads. To emphasise its now permanent place and the status of this remarkable event in the cultural calendar of Scotland, it was decided that a symbolic statement was required. The Tattoo, while very much the newcomer, had proved its popularity, and what better location was there available for a one-off celebration than the Castle Esplanade at the heart of Scotland's Capital.

Thus, on the last night of the Edinburgh Festival of 1950, with Queen Elizabeth and Princess Margaret in attendance, took place an experience that nobody present would ever forget.

Under the illuminated tip of the baton of the legendary Sir Thomas Beecham, founder of the Royal Philharmonic Orchestra, the combined military bands of The Royal Scots (The Royal Regiment), The Royal Scots Greys, The 9th Queen's Royal Lancers and The

2.2 HM The Queen and HRH Princess Margaret attend the 1950 Tattoo

Highland Light Infantry, augmented by eight double basses from the Royal Philharmonic Orchestra, gave a performance of Handel's *Music for the Royal Fireworks* to the accompaniment of canon, twenty-five pounders from the Saluting Battery on Mills Mount, high up on the Castle ramparts.

The staging was immaculate. The impact breathtaking. The music was followed by a display of fireworks, after which the performers taking part, The Brigade of Guards, the Highland dancers, and troops wearing the uniform of the 79th Highlanders of the year 1828, formed up in position, towards the lower end of the Esplanade, with the massed pipes and drums to the rear. In appropriate manner, the Lord Provost thanked the artistes, his fellow citizens and all who had taken part. The Edinburgh Festival and the Edinburgh Military Tattoo were here to stay.

In his memoires, *One Blue Bonnet*, the former Major, by then Brigadier, Frank Coutts had the following recollection of the event:

> At the afternoon rehearsals Beecham said to the Artillery officer, 'Now your cue to fire the guns is the only time I will raise my baton in the air and point it right at you up on the ramparts.' Unfortunately he didn't give the poor Gunner time to walk back up to his post. When it came to the 'moment critique' the guns did not roar out. Sir Thomas dropped his baton and put his hand up to his ear. The orchestra hooted with laughter. Everything went fine on the night.

And as those guns cracked out from the ancient castle battlements, they symbolised not only the ending of an era, but a new beginning for the hopes and aspirations of all the British people embarking upon the second half of the twentieth century. It was, so far as everybody involved was concerned, a triumph.

In those first three years of the Edinburgh Festival, the financing of the military presentations was on a very small scale. By today's standards it seems absurd. In 1947 an expenditure of £637 produced

£1,044 of income. By 1949, income of £3,492 was taken in for an expenditure of £2,113. By the early 1950s, as might have been expected, expenditure rose substantially, including by this time the cost of spectator stand erection and dismantling. By 1954, expenditure was of the order of £45,000 with an income of £65,700.

About this time a regular pattern of distribution of the surplus income of some £20,500 emerged. £7,500 was allocated to service charities, and £11,000 to the Edinburgh Festival Society, with the balance of £2,000 put in reserve.

The understanding upon which the military authorities and Edinburgh Corporation appeared to work for some years thereafter was that the surplus proceeds should be distributed equally to service charities and to the Corporation's charitable institution, namely the Edinburgh Festival Society after a small augmentation of the Tattoo Reserve Fund had been creamed off.

A lot of lessons can be learned from that original partnership in an age when agreements were binding and people bonded together to make things work. On the City side, Sir John Imrie, the City Chamberlain, appointed Thomas K. Currie, known to his colleagues as 'TK', the Assistant City Chamberlain, to take charge of all the administrative and financial arrangements. This involved a major input by many staff within the City Chamberlain's Department. And altogether, Tom Currie's contribution to the early years of the Tattoo was invaluable. Cecil Stout recalled him as follows:

Tom Currie was very popular and friendly both as a person and as a senior official. His charisma was such that virtually anyone of his acquaintance would undertake voluntary work for him.

And thus it was that the first Tattoo stewards came principally from male staff of various departments of Edinburgh Corporation and rugby enthusiasts used to stewarding at Murrayfield, Edinburgh's rugby ground. The City Chamberlain's Department was an extremely versatile one being blessed with highly competent female staff comprising comptometer operators, typists and book-keepers. These young ladies (collectively known as 'The Machine Room') quickly created and managed the systems required for the sale and financial control of tickets whilst T.K. supervised the whole operation with the support of his secretary.

Male members of the Department's staff took over after office hours during the Tattoo period to organise the control of the small army of stewards and programme sellers as well as the sale of tickets for the evening performance, and generally the handling of cash with which they were familiar.

To this day the support of volunteer stewards who come from all walks of life continues. Many have turned out every night each year for over twenty years and their contribution to the overall safety and enjoyment of the event is unparalleled for its dedication.

The City Chamberlain's Department at the City Chambers in the High Street became the front-of-house administrative centre, whilst the production centre of the Tattoo was situated up the road at Edinburgh Castle. The comings and goings of uniformed servicemen became a regular sight around the City Chambers in those early years.

Spotlights had to be hired in since Army searchlights worked off generators which made far too much noise. Jim Tweedie, a senior architect, was appointed by the City Architect to undertake drawings, oversee technical matters, and to create some form of elevated seating. It had been obvious from the start that the steep slope of the Esplanade would make it necessary for some sort of stand provision if spectators were to be properly accommodated. Initially two small ad hoc stands were provided on the North and South side. In later years the stands grew in size, and the East Stand acquired a Royal Box. Initially a few rows of chairs were provided in front of the stands, but as the stands grew in size, the chairs were discounted as their encroachment onto the Esplanade was considered unacceptable. Slowly, and methodically, the organisation machine for the Edinburgh Military Tattoo began to materialise on an annual basis into its current highly geared and efficient structure. Looking back from this age of technology to those early days it might seem incredible that there were no serious mishaps or behind-the-scenes disasters. Nevertheless, it also speaks volumes about the commitment of all those dedicated men and women who were so determined that the show must go on.

# 3 Forward March

EMPHASISING the importance of youth in the modern army, the Feu de Joie which commenced the 1951 programme was followed by Tomorrow's Men, a performance which featured Highland dancing by boys of the Queen Victoria School, Dunblane, accompanied by the pipes and drums, 1st Battalion The Seaforth Highlanders. The mounted band of The Royal Horse Guards ('The Blues'), under their Director of Music Captain David McBain, appeared for the first time, followed by a pageant depicting incidents from the history of the Scottish Priory of the Order of the Knights of St John of Jerusalem.

A musical display entitled 'From the Bens and the Glens' for the first time brought together the pipes and drums of The 1st Battalion The Royal Scots (The Royal Regiment), 1st Battalion The Royal Scots Fusiliers, 1st Battalion The Black Watch (Royal Highland Regiment), 1st Battalion The Seaforth Highlanders (Ross-shire Buffs) and the Argyll and Sutherland Highlanders of Canada. Marches included *Green Hills of Tyrol*, *Heroes of Vittoria*, *Skye Boat Song* and *Blue Bonnets Over the Border*.

3.1 The 1951 programme cover. A.E. Haswell Miller provided the illustrations for the early covers

EDINBURGH    FESTIVAL    1951

*Scottish Command*

*presents*

*The*

*Edinburgh*

*Tattoo*

1951

*at the Castle*

Produced by LIEUT.-COLONEL G. I. MALCOLM OF POLTALLOCH

PROGRAMME
Price 1/-

The seating was increased to accommodate 7,000 per performance, and it was estimated afterwards that the overall attendance had grown to 160,000 as a result. And this was the year when outside television broadcasting arrived in Scotland. According to BBC producer Ian Christie, the cost of that first Tattoo production was an astonishing £200.

Aubrey Singer, who later became BBC Television's Managing Director, was the producer of the first televised Tattoo performance, and the day after the broadcast he received a memo from the Head of BBC Television Films to compliment him on 'the restrained and informative commentary'. The technical excellence of the pictures, he was told, was 'beyond all criticism'.

As a result of this, an era of mass exposure was about to begin for the Edinburgh Tattoo. The Royal Marines mounted a drill display by recruits of less than seventeen weeks, and the massed bands under the direction of Captain W. Lang of The Royal Marines played *Garb of Old Gaul*, *Stars and Stripes Forever*, *Scotland the Brave* and *Colonel Bogey* to a captivated audience across the country and beyond.

The applause was tumultuous and the reputation of the Tattoo had been growing with each performance. Then, quite unexpectedly, George Malcolm, the man who had made it all happen, announced his departure. Robin Malcolm is on record as saying that he can only guess at his father's reasons. They never discussed it, he said, but it is clearly apparent that the job had grown from part-time to full-time, and by this stage George Malcolm had begun to take a more active interest in his Argyllshire land. That taken into account, the most likely explanation for his decision to opt out is simply that, being the perfectionist he was, it was becoming increasingly difficult for him to allocate sufficient hours and energy to both jobs at the same time.

Poltalloch House, the enormous Victorian mansion which the Malcolm family had occupied since 1850, was in such disrepair that it had finally been decided to pull it down. The family intended to move into Duntrune Castle, a twelfth century fortress they had acquired from Clan Campbell in 1792, but never occupied.

However, first there needed to be extensive renovations, a modern kitchen and bathrooms. A great deal of work was required to make it habitable, and for the laird to be on the spot had become essential.

George Malcolm was aged forty-eight, and as a farmer, despite his earlier lack of expertise, was to acquire a reputation for breeding part-bred Arab ponies. He also wrote several books on the history of The Argyll and Sutherland Highlanders plus the official history of the Argyllshire Gathering, the west coast Highland games event which dates back to 1872.

However, there was only one problem. It might have been assumed that with his intimate involvement and undoubted enthusiasm, Alasdair Maclean would immediately step into the breach, but this was impossible. Although he no doubt wanted to, Maclean was still a serving officer attached to Scottish Command and unable officially to take over the full-time role of producer, or pageant master, as the role was described in the programme. And that is why the twenty-five year-old Captain Forbes Taylor, late of The Black Watch (Royal Highland Regiment), quite unexpectedly found himself as producer and stage manager for one year only.

In 1948 Taylor had helped George Malcolm to stage a 'Services Cavalcade' in the Kelvin Hall, Glasgow. It had been a try-out for a possible northern Royal Tournament, considered an important initiative at the time and one which had indirectly led to the Tattoo. Taylor's experience working in Glasgow therefore made him extremely capable of doing the job and certainly the experience proved invaluable when he later moved on to a busy and successful career in films and television production.

That year the salute was taken by HRH The Duke of Edinburgh, the third member of the Royal Family to attend the Tattoo officially, and it was as if the public just could not get enough of it.

There is something profoundly moving about the sight and sound of a military parade. The Scots, with such a long standing tradition of military service, and boasting some of the United Kingdom's oldest regiments, have it deeply embedded in their psyche, which perhaps explains why the Edinburgh Tattoo has outlasted even the Royal Tournament.

In 1952, there was a pageant entitled 'Scotland in Arms', which illustrated the changes in dress of all the Scottish Regiments from the seventeenth to the twentieth century. The biggest cheer was for the 1914 contingent which entered through a cloud of smoke led by a piper of the Cameronians (Scottish Rifles). Far greater changes were afoot for the Scottish Regiments, but the themes even then were deeply symbolic.

For the first time in 1952 there were guest performers from overseas, the Pipes and Drums of the 1st Canadian Highland Battalion was a composite unit formed for service in Germany. Canada until then had no permanent armed forces, and the Canadian pipes and drums formed part of the Massed Pipes and Drums along with the 1st and 2nd Battalions Scots Guards, The 2nd Battalion Black Watch, The 1st Seaforth and The 1st Cameron Highlanders. From France came La Fanfare à Cheval de La Garde Republicaine de Paris, directed by Trumpet-Major Gossez; from Holland, The Koninklijke Militaire Kapel (Royal Netherlands Grenadiers), under their Director of Music, Captain R. Van Yperen. Three National Anthems were played at the end of the evening, *Wilhelmus Van Nassau*, *La Marseillaise* and *God Save The Queen*.

3.2 1952 programme cover

The arrival of these overseas participants was very much a foretaste of what was to come. As the prestige of the Edinburgh International Festival gathered momentum, with the Tattoo an integral part of the concept, the news spread around the world and invitations began to arrive for the Tattoo producer to visit military and associated events in other countries.

3.3 A display from the 1952 Tattoo

What was even more remarkable is that from the very beginning overseas performers wishing to participate in the Tattoo were made aware that they would be expected to pay their own expenses. While accommodation was provided, regiments and bands who were invited by the producer, after strict scrutiny of their abilities and appeal, were obliged to make their own travel arrangements. Far from discouraging them, the honour of being invited to take part in an Edinburgh Tattoo came increasingly to be seen as a distinctive accolade.

# 4　An Outstanding Showman

BORN in Lochbuie Castle on the island of Mull in 1902, Alasdair Gillean Lorne Maclean served with The Queen's Own Cameron Highlanders for thirty-three years after training at Sandhurst. There were postings in Burma and Japan, and at various times he served as A.D.C. to two Viceroys of India. During World War Two he commanded the 1st Cameron Highlanders in Japan and Malaya, and later became Assistant Adjutant General, Scottish Command.

An outstanding Highland dancer, Lieutenant Colonel Maclean, who took the rank of Brigadier when he officially left the army, became chairman of the Scottish Official Board of Highland Dancing. His achievements in this field were commemorated in 1963 with a tune written especially in his honour entitled, *Alasdair Maclean's Reel*. Intensely proud of his West Highland ancestry, he was also President of the Clan Maclean Society in Edinburgh.

This then was the background to the man whom the army appointed Director of the first full-blown Edinburgh Military Tattoo when it was proposed for 1950. He was therefore not only ideally positioned, but temperamentally inclined to take over the reigns when George Malcolm departed as Producer two years later, but since, as has already been explained, that had simply not been possible, he had to wait until 1953.

'He was a West Highland Cameron and totally unpredictable,' recalled Lieutenant Colonel Bobby Smith, former Adjutant at Edinburgh Castle. 'A good piper and an expert dancer, and above all an outstanding showman and commentator. He was a dedicated

4.1 Brigadier Alasdair Maclean

'Scot' and understood the audiences, especially the ones that came from the West. His use of the vernacular and sudden switches to the "couthy" were masterly.'

When in 1953 Maclean began producing the Tattoo, he also took upon himself a variety of other responsibilities such as the commentary, and in 1955 took the Edinburgh Tattoo in its entirety to Copenhagen, paid for by the British Chamber of Commerce, and accompanied by his chairman, Major General Victor Campbell, chief of staff Scottish Command.

Eleven years later in 1964, the Brigadier set off to Australia with the pipes and drums of three Scottish regiments to perform at the Sydney Tattoo. 'Unlike the wanderlust Macleans, I want the world to come to me,' he once remarked.

In his memoirs *One Blue Bonnet*, Brigadier Frank Coutts, former Colonel of the King's Own Scottish Borderers, an assistant-commentator at the Tattoo and Chairman of the Tattoo Committee from 1967 to 1968, made the following observation, with an additional insight into a behind the scenes hiccup:

That great character – lovable, maddening – Lieutenant Colonel Alasdair Maclean of Pennycross (don't ever get the Pennycross wrong) was on the staff of headquarters as Assistant Adjutant General and it was he who lifted the Tattoo from being a side-show in Princes Street Gardens to the famous international spectacle which it is today. As soon as the TA camps were over everyone in the headquarters was involved in some way. I started as 'dog's body' to Alasdair and, over the years, became his assistant and commentator in several Tattoos during the fifties.

They were much more amateur in those days – although there were far more troops involved than today. There were problems galore, but everyone enjoyed being part of a theatrical show once a year. One night when the Admiral was taking the salute, the audience gasped when the Senior Drum Major came out of the castle and over the drawbridge staggering all over the place, completely 'fu'. We had to endure this staggering performance right down the Esplanade and up again. To his eternal credit, he never dropped his mace. Alasdair, Bob Happer, Douglas Spratt (lights) and I were really busy on the phone. While the bands were counter marching at the top of the Esplanade, the lights were directed elsewhere. The Military Police emerged unseen from the Castle and when the lights came on again the 'Drummie' wasn't there. He was in durance vile. Considering the number of troops involved there were very few dramas of that kind.

Brigadier Maclean's first Tattoo as Producer took place two months after the Coronation of Queen Elizabeth II. The Tattoo included two massed Pipes and Drums, one Scottish and one from the Commonwealth, as well as the Massed Pipes and Drums of The Brigade of Gurkhas who had a separate 'slot'. The Commonwealth Pipe Band included the Pipes and Drums of The 1st Gordon Highlanders with pipers from The Royal Inniskilling and The Royal Irish Fusiliers together with representatives of Commonwealth countries who had played with the Massed Pipes and Drums in the Coronation procession – The Pipe Band of the 8th Punjab Regiment from Pakistan plus pipers from The New Zealand Scottish, the Kimberley Regiment from South Africa, and two battalions of The Black Watch of Canada. The action 'item' featured the capture and rescue of the Scottish outlaw hero Rob Roy MacGregor from the Fort at Inversnaid.

Among the regiments that had taken part in the Coronation Parade in London had been the Gurkhas, who made the first of their many Tattoo appearances with a sixty-strong pipe band and a drill squad. On this occasion, performers were drawn from The 2nd (King Edward's Own) Gurkha Rifles, 6th Gurkha Rifles, 7th Gurkha Rifles and 10th (Princess Mary's Own) Gurkha Rifles. Originally raised in 1815 in Nepal by the British East India Company, these Gurkha regiments had retained a particularly fine record as fighting men, winning no less than twelve of the thirty-six Victoria Crosses awarded to the Indian Army during World War Two. In 1948, when India became independent, it was agreed that four Battalions of the Gurkha Brigade should be transferred to the British Army.

4.2  The Royal Gurkha Rifles have been staunch participants in the Tattoo

Nineteen fifty-three was also the first of many Tattoos for Major Jimmy Howe of the Scots Guards, who became bandmaster of the Argyll and Sutherland Highlanders. Living in married quarters at Dreghorn, at the foot of the Pentland Hills, and overlooking the city, his wife could see the floodlights of the Castle going out at the end of each performance, and this was her cue for putting on the kettle and preparing supper. 'It never failed,' she said. 'He would always arrive home to find the food on the table.'

By this stage, George Malcolm's son Robin was also serving with The 1st Argyll and Sutherland Highlanders and had arrived at Redford Barracks as the regiment's newest National Service officer. Since his colleagues were mostly either involved in the Tattoo, or in the north of Scotland guarding the Royal Family at Balmoral Castle in Aberdeenshire, he was appointed semi-permanent orderly officer, which meant that he was responsible for turning out the Castle Guard when it was the Argyll's turn to supply it.

During one scene, a redcoat was seen being hurled from the battlements by a muscular Highlander, with the dummy retrieved from the moat night after night. The unsuspecting Robin recalled arriving around 3am to inspect the guard only to have his attention distracted by an unmistakably dead redcoat in a corner, an experience which was to prompt visions of endless fatal accident procedures for the remainder of his two years at Redford. He had fallen straight into the trap laid by that scheming guard!

It was the first time at the Tattoo that the Brigadier had arranged for mounted bands to take part, followed in later years by other 'Household' mounted bands and also mounted bands from France and the Middle East. For past performances, horses had been borrowed from Spylaw Riding Academy, Jack Cullen of Newbridge Farm and St Cuthbert's Co-Operative Society, but from now on the regiments brought their own.

4.3

To start off with, the regimental horses which arrived at Gorgie Market Railway Siding were stabled at Redford Cavalry Barracks, at Colinton, on the outskirts of the city. This was a fair trek back and forth to the Esplanade, so eventually it was arranged with St Cuthbert's Co-op to make use of its stables at Gardeners Crescent, Fountainbridge.

It was exactly this sort of situation that needed to be thought out in precise detail beforehand. Moreover, the weather needed always to be taken into account. While waiting for their performance, the mounted bands would occupy Parliament Square beside St Giles's Cathedral and when the wind and the rain whipped up it could become highly unpleasant. After an early experience of just how bad this could be, temporary canvas shelters were erected to provide some cover particularly during double performances. Subsequently these were provided within the castle walls.

The Mounted Band of the Royal Horse Guards (The Blues), stationed at Windsor, took part in the Tattoo in 1954 for the first and last time, playing under the direction of Captain J.E. Thirtle. A former director of music had been Major David McBain, a native of Edinburgh who during the 1930s had written a stirring march for bugles and military band entitled *Mechanised Infantry*, played many times over the years to follow and which had become a popular march in the repertoire of The Royal Marines, The Light Infantry and The Royal Green Jackets.

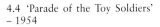
4.4 'Parade of the Toy Soldiers'
– 1954

David McBain had three sons, two of them twins, all of whom were commissioned into Scottish Regiments. Two years earlier Stuart, the elder twin, having a few months earlier joined The Royal Scots, had found himself commanding a platoon of Pikemen, part of the display put on by The Lowland Brigade who were dressed in uniforms covering four centuries. The Tattoo was becoming a real family affair.

And always there was an element of recruitment, with the emphasis firmly on youth. Forty-eight cadets from the Royal Military Academy, Sandhurst, gave a drill display, while one hundred boys of 'B' Company, 1st Regular Training Battalion, The Royal Army Ordnance Corps under Captain D.F.A. Cowdry provided a Parade of the Toy Soldiers. A physical training display was put on by boys of the Army Apprentice School, Harrogate under Major H.N. Clemas of The Duke of Cornwall's Light Infantry. A team of eighty Highland dancers from six regiments joined up with boys from the Queen Victoria School, Dunblane to give a display accompanied by the Pipes and Drums of The Queen's Own Cameron Highlanders.

The Producer, while all this was going on, appeared indomitable. Brigadier Coutts recalled how one day he was summoned to Alasdair's bedside at his home in Lennox Street to be told that he was not well. Mary Maclean escorted him to the bedroom where the Brigadier said to him, 'I can't possibly make it tonight, Frank. I have complete faith in you, carry on.'

Half an hour before the start, Coutts remembers seeing Maclean arrive in a City Council staff car from which he was carried on a litter to the Producer's Box.

'How are you feeling, Sir?' shouted the press who surrounded him.

'Just a touch of myxomatosis!' he responded.

'That's the Brigadier for you,' commented a colleague.

# 5  Rugged on the Nylons

BY the end of the 1950s, the input from overseas visitors continued to be increasingly significant. As the Edinburgh Festival developed into the largest cultural event of its kind in the world, the audiences for the Tattoo became progressively more cosmopolitan.

And this was reflected in the star attractions it featured, each in some way translating into a history of the lands of their origin. For example, a random selection included The 16th Battalion, Australian Military Forces (The Cameron Highlanders of Western Australia), The Pipe Band of The 8th Punjab Regiment from Pakistan, The 1st Armoured Car Regiment Band from New Zealand. From the Union of South Africa came The Kimberley Regiment, formed in 1899, and The Witwatersrand Rifles, first recruited from mining employees in West Rand in 1903.

The Black Watch (Royal Highland Regiment) of Canada was first raised in 1862 as The 5th Battalion Royal Light Infantry, but in 1880 became The Royal Scots Fusiliers of Canada, in 1906 The Royal Highlanders of Canada, and in 1930 took its current title. During World War One it saw service in France and Flanders, when four members of the

5.1

Regiment won the Victoria Cross. During World War Two, the Black Watch of Canada served in north-west Europe, taking part in all the campaigns of Second Canadian Infantry Division. In 1951, two battalions of the Regiment were incorporated in the Canadian Regular Army. Both were to see service in Germany post-war, and the 2nd battalion was based in Korea from 1953-54.

The King's African Rifles was formed in 1902 from units in the East African, Central African, and Ugandan Rifles. In those days before the excesses of Colonel Idi Amin and Ugandan Independence, with Her Majesty the Queen as Colonel-in-Chief, the regiment comprised the 1st and 2nd Nyasaland Battalions, The 3rd, 2/3rd, 5th, 11th Kenya, 4th Uganda and 6th and 2/6th Tanganyika, names now lost in the passage of time.

During the State of Emergency in neighbouring Kenya, the Askaris of The King's African Rifles were in action against Mau Mau terrorists from 1952 until November 1956 without respite. Trackers by instinct, with an acute sense of hearing, sight and smell, they moved through Kenya's tangled forests with a natural skill which only years of special training could have instilled.

Another great success was The Royal Canadian Mounted Police, formed in 1873 as The North-West Mounted Police to provide protection in the unsettled portions of north-west Canada. In 1904, the prefix of 'Royal' was added, and in 1920, when the Dominion Police was amalgamated with this force, the name was again changed, this time to its present form. Headquarters were moved from Regina to Ottowa, and by 1928 had absorbed the Saskatchewan Provincial Police Force. Four years later the Provincial Police Forces in Alberta, Manitoba, New Brunswick, Nova Scotia and Prince Edward Island were similarly incorporated, and in 1950 the duties of the Newfoundland Rangers and certain members of the Newfoundland Constabulary were taken over.

Then there was the first appearance of Turkish soldiers at a foreign Tattoo. The Corps of Janissaries, once feared throughout the whole of Western Europe, had been originally formed as a bodyguard for the Sultan of Turkey, recruited from Christians and other slaves in the

5.2 The Royal Canadian Mounted Police have been associated with the Tattoo for many years; they are seen here in 2000

Ottoman Empire. The founder was Sultan Orkhan (1326-59), but the real organiser of the Corps as an elite regiment and royal bodyguard was Orkhan's successor, Sultan Murad I, who was the conqueror of the Balkan Peninsula. The Janissaries, although Christians converted to Islam, soon became noted for their fanatical loyalty to the Sultan, and they enjoyed many privileges as a result.

At first the Janissaries had only comprised 2,000 men, but by the seventeenth century they numbered 200,000. By this time, the Janissaries had become so powerful in the Ottoman Empire that they were often in a position to overthrow the reigning Sultans, and it became inevitable that eventually the reforming Sultan Mahmud II

(1808-39) would finally disband what had become a permanent menace to the Imperial Throne.

Only recently therefore had the Janissaries' Band been revived for military parades and dressed in authentic costumes with traditional intruments. They were joined by cadets from Harp Okulu, or the Turkish Military Academy, established in Istanbul in 1834 to train regular officers for the Turkish Army in the European military tradition. Mustafa Kemel Ataturk, the World War One Turkish General, for fifteen years Turkey's President, was one of the cadets who graduated from Harp Okulu with the requisite degree of proficiency.

One Scandinavian regiment in particular, however, was to distinguish itself in the most unexpected way, and this was the Royal Danish Life Guards.

The journalist Gordon Dean was working as a reporter with the *Daily Record* in the branch office in Frederick Street, off Princes Street, from where the searchlight operators could be seen doing their dazzling best on the castle rock.

'The rehearsal had been in progress for an hour when, as the Royal Danish Lifeguards marched on to the Esplanade, flames suddenly appeared under some seats on the North Stand,' he wrote the following day. 'A back cloth of tarpaulins had caught alight and soon the flames were leaping some twenty feet above the spectators.

'A passer-by rushed into the *Record* office and shouted to us, "The Tattoo's on fire!" We hurried outside into the street and quickly saw that it was no leg-pull, so immediately our photographer grabbed his equipment and raced up the Mound.'

Meanwhile on the Castle Esplanade itself, a dramatic two-word order by a Danish naval officer instantly quelled what had looked like a nasty situation and prevented panic among the stand's 3,000 spectators in the wooden platform seats as the flames leaped dangerously close.

The officer was in charge of eighty ratings from a Danish ship anchored in the Forth. When the fire started in the canvas wind

5.3 'Cavalcade of the Lowland Brigade' – The Royal Scots of 1633 are in the foreground. The year is 1955

barrier behind the stand, he calmly ordered his men to remain where they were. Meanwhile, on the Esplanade, the Life Guards stood stoically to attention.

The sailors from the frigate *Holger Danske* kept their seats until the crowds in the rows in front of them had been evacuated. Then they helped army personnel cut down the blazing tarpaulins which fell into the gardens below. The drama was over. Forty minutes after the fire started, the crowd were making their way back to their seats. In true entertainment tradition, the show went on, and there were cheers for the Danish sailors and soldiers for helping prevent what could have been a major catastrophe.

In 1958, a commercial sound recording was attempted, and Bryce Laing of Craighall Sound Productions recalled that two 'Ball and Biscuit' microphones (so called because of their distinctive appearance) were used. 'They were slung across the arena about a quarter and three quarters of the way down from the drawbridge. The results were sufficiently acceptable to produce and issue for sale a ten inch mono long playing record.'

Laing, a wartime Cameronian who was awarded a Military Medal, was to become involved in recording the sound of the Tattoo for some forty years, and to this day provides invaluable advice in the context of the annual recorded musical content. But it was not until 1961, when recording equipment and expertise had dramatically improved, that the first twelve inch stereo LP record was issued, although recordings of the 1959 and 1960 Tattoos were also made, albeit still as ten inch Monos.

However, the late 1950s did mark that burgeoning period when television pictures first started being transmitted across the English Channel and millions of viewers in Europe were able to join the by then dedicated following that the Tattoo had attracted in Britain. When video recording was introduced during the mid-1960s, tapes of the event were flown to many countries around the world. In Australia it is still said that 'Ne'erday just wouldn't be the same without the annual Tattoo broadcast.'

Celebrities of stage and screen came too, to see for themselves. Some were appearing in shows at the Festival, others had simply come

5.4 Scottish country dancers became firm favourites with Tattoo audiences

to spectate. Among them were Douglas Fairbanks Junior, Googie Withers, and the Canadian actress Yvonne de Carlo, who became fascinated with the knives the kilted soldiers wore in the tops of their socks.

'They are called sgian dubh,' explained Alasdair Maclean, mischievously adding, 'We use them for defending ourselves, and Scottish girls often carry them too.

'Gee, Brigadier. That must be rugged on the nylons,' she responded.

# 6   The Swinging Sixties

THE dawning of the new decade found Alasdair Maclean the dominant force behind increasingly ambitious Tattoo programmes, although there was a certain occurrence that has remained in the psyche of officianados ever since.

During the early years, the catering arrangements for the troops were, to be blunt, a bit primitive. Performers received a packed meal assembled by the army caterers. Every night there was an orange included and, recorded freelance journalist David Ben-Aryeah at the time, 'after twenty performances the boys and girls were getting a bit sick of oranges'.

On the last performance, therefore, just as the massed bands struck up for the final display, wave after wave of oranges, in perfect formation, rolled down the gentle slop of the Esplanade, every bandsman having taken a couple to release 'in tempo.'

'The point was well made,' recorded Ben-Aryeah. 'Next year, NO ORANGES.'

Otherwise, of course, everything went splendidly. Visitors included the 7th Regiment of Spahis, the survivors of the magnificent French/Arab mounted regiments created by General Yusuf at the time of the conquest of Algeria. Mounted on their Barbary stallions, the Spahis evoked exotic memories of the magnificent cavalry of old.

From Greece came the Greek Royal Guard who, apart from a handful of officers and NCOs, were exclusively required to be over six feet tall. Coincidentally their uniform consisted of a kilt (foustanella) in continuation of the magnificent Hellenic uniform worn by the first Greek freedom fighters.

Soldiers representing Canada were much in evidence. The Corps of the Royal Canadian Engineers, The Lorne Scots (Peel, Dufferin and Halton) Regiment wearing the ancient Campbell of Argyll tartan, The Queen's Own Rifles of Canada, the oldest regiment in the Canadian Regular Army, and returning after seven years, The Pipes and Drums of the 2nd Battalion, The Black Watch (Royal Highland Regiment) of Canada to celebrate its one hundredth anniversary.

With the outbreak of the European war in 1940, HM Kongens Garde (His Majesty the King's Norwegian Guard) under King Haakon VII of Norway had participated valiantly in the fighting at Elverum, Strandlykja and Lundehogda. However, post-war, the most surprising aspect of this startlingly brisk and colourful company was the length of service required of its men. Considering the professionalism they displayed at concerts, and in drills and parades, it might have been expected they had all undergone years of tough training, but as it transpired, their period of service was only nine months.

6.1 HM Kongens Garde outside the Royal Palace, Oslo

Admittedly, when the invitation to attend the Edinburgh Military Tattoo of 1961 arrived, the company commander had pushed forward his drill programme, but it was certainly not obvious from the discipline of the contingent that came to Scotland consisting of fifty musicians in the band, eighteen drummers and buglers in the signal corps, thirty-six riflemen, and eleven officers. Possibly they had been forewarned, because Major Nils Egelien, platoon commander, said that he would never forget Brigadier Maclean's voice coming over the loud speaker as they practiced their ski patrol demonstration. 'Royal Norwegian Guard,' boomed the Brigadier. 'You are five seconds too late. Please repeat!'

Nils Egelien was to forge an important diplomatic link during that visit. On an outing to Edinburgh Zoo, he discovered that the zoo penguins had originally been brought from the Arctic by Lord Salvesen, a member of the Norwegian whaling and shipping family which had established itself in Scotland in 1843. When HM Kongens Garde returned to Edinburgh in 1972, they adopted one of these penguins and named him Nils Olav, after Major Egelien and King Olav, bestowing upon the bird the rank of lance corporal.

On the next visit, Lance Corporal Nils Olav was promoted to sergeant and thereafter marched daily at the front of the Zoo's Penguin Parade, a fine representative of the Royal Norwegian Guard.

Shortly after Indian independence in 1947, the military forces of the princely states were reorganised and amalgamated into the Indian Army. The cavalry units or detachments maintained by some of the states merged to form one regiment, and as a result, the 61st Cavalry Regiment was raised in November 1953. The major portion was formed by men coming from the Jodhpur Sardar Risala, Kachawa Horse (Jaipur), Mysor Lancers, and Gwalior Lancers.

Although reformed, the 61st Cavalry inherited the traditions of its predecessors. The Rajput element stemmed from the units which at heavy odds had fought valiantly against the Moguls in places such as Chittor and Haldighat. The Mysore Lancers were formed from the remnants of Tippoo Sultan's Cavalry following the Battle of Seringapatam.

In World War One, the Jodhpur Sardar Risala and the Mysore Lancers took part in what was one of the last cavalry charges in modern military history and performing for the first time at Edinburgh Castle were Rajputs, Rajasthanis, Muslims (Kaim Khanis) from Rajasthan, and Maharattas from Maharashtra. It was a remarkable sight, and complementing the 61st Cavalry in 1962 was the 15th Ludhiana Sikhs, the 2nd Battalion The Sikh Regiment, which since its formation in 1846 had gained twenty Battle Honours in various theatres of war from China to Europe. To date it had won an impressive 301 honours and awards including two Victoria Crosses and two Ashoka Chakras Class 1.

The links between Britain and Jordan were equally strong, and from Amman came The Pipes and Drums of the Royal Jordan Arab Army under the direction of Captain Saleh Baghdadi, Director of Music. It was another unforgettable experience.

In 1920, a British soldier, Captain F.G. Peake, had raised the Arab Legion to establish public security in the new state of Transjordan, and to keep the unruly local tribes in order. To begin with, it had been only 200 strong, but by 1921 had grown to comprise two companies of infantry, two squadrons of cavalry, a troop of artillery and a signals section. The Civil Police were also under its command.

6.2 & 6.3 A contrast in styles (*left*) a sailors' hornpipe and (*right*) the audience was encouraged to come on to the Castle Esplanade to demonstrate the Twist

In 1927, Britain signed a treaty and guaranteed to defend Transjordan against external aggression, which effectively made the Legion redundant, but when Major J.B. Glubb was given orders to end tribal raiding, he raised a desert patrol of ninety men, and between 1931 and 1936, the Legion was gradually expanded and found itself in control of a country the size of Scotland.

When the Transjordan Frontier Force was disbanded in 1948, some of the personnel joined the Arab Legion. Thereafter, it had continued to expand, especially after it changed its name to the Royal Jordan Arab Army under the command of the young and popular King Hussein.

By this stage, Alasdair Maclean was travelling extensively, and all kinds of continental musical treats were in evidence. For example, there was the Bagad of Lann-Bihoue from Brittany, only twelve years old, having been formed with the help of French naval authorities, who had in the first instance recruited Breton pipers on duty at the Naval Air Station in northern France. In 1960, the Bagad had won first prize at an international competition of pipers at Brest, and its repertoire included Celtic folklore tunes and marches written by contemporary Breton composers.

Then there was the Isle of Barbados Police Band. Proud of its British heritage, the Barbados Police came into being only six years after the first Metropolitan Police Force in England. The band, which at the Tattoo had Bernard Morris as its acting bandmaster, had been originally established by a Mr Willocks, bandmaster of the British Regiment then stationed in Barbados, and thus the scarlet braid on the caps and trousers of the bandsmen came to be copied from the uniforms of British regiments stationed in Barbados during the reign of Queen Victoria.

From Fiji, then still a British Colony, came the Band of the Fiji Military Force which had come into being when a shipment of brass instruments was sent to Suva, the capital, in 1919. The small band which then formed gave its first concert on Christmas Day of that year. It flourished, was broken up on the outbreak of World War

Two, but reformed and was employed on stretcher-bearer duties with the 1st Battalion of the Fiji Infantry Regiment. During the Solomons Campaign in the South Pacific, its Bandmaster was awarded the Military Cross, and a bandsman won the Military Medal.

Like all South Sea Islanders, Fijians, though lacking in formal musical education, were naturally musical. A novel instrument which does not appear in other bands was the derua, a hollow length of bamboo which, when banged vertically on the ground, produces a sound, and for the duration of the 1965 Tattoo, the Fijians delighted audiences with their traditional dances called mekes (pronounced 'meckee'), discarding their colourful uniforms of scarlet tunics and white sulus or long kilts for coloured native costumes.

# 7 Come to the Dance

THE Brigadier was a showman who understood that there was more to military extravaganzas than bands and marching men. Following the example of the Royal Tournament, he believed that a Tattoo should also be about action and physical prowess, but above all it was about entertainment.

A typical example was when he acquired the world-famous James Bond Aston Martin car for use in a demonstration by Royal Marine Commandos entitled 'Operation 007'. Freelance journalist David Ben-Aryeah recalled how on a very wet night it lost control and gracefully slid into the front of the east stand. 'The press officer that night did one of the fastest disappearing acts ever witnessed,' he wrote.

The South Eastern Fire Brigade made its Tattoo debut in 1963 to demonstrate its expertise by rescuing damsels from the flame-engulfed battlements, and holding a competition between fire engine crews which culminated in a coloured water display. With thirty-two stations, the South Eastern Fire Brigade then consisted of Edinburgh and all the brigades in the seven surrounding counties which had been brought together in 1948. The only professional member in this consortium at the time was Edinburgh.

This had singular historic significance. Chief Officers of Fire Brigades in Scotland are called Firemasters, and the title was first employed in Edinburgh in 1703. The first municipal Fire Brigade in the world was formed in Edinburgh in 1824, under the command of James Braidwood who later became Chief Officer of the London Fire

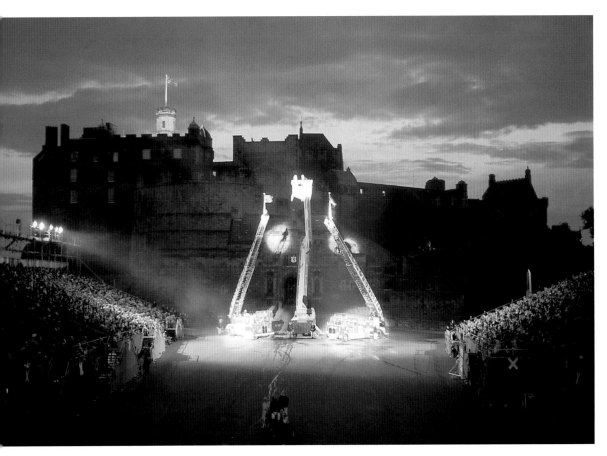

7.1 A fire-fighting display

Engines Establishment which ultimately became London Fire Brigade. Coincidentally, F. Rushbrook, the S.E.F.B.'s Firemaster in 1964, had started his career in the Edinburgh Fire Brigade, eventually becoming Chief Officer of East Ham, London, before returning to Edinburgh to complete the cycle.

In 1964, there was a demonstration of Scottish dancing by the British Columbia Highland Lassies from Vancouver. Mary Isdale, a Canadian Scot, had made an extensive study of Highland dancing and amassed a collection of over one hundred dances since emigrating from her native Govan, in Glasgow. These had been published by the Royal Scottish Country Dance Society, and this was the second time she had worked with Alasdair Maclean, having taken part in the

Vancouver Tattoo which he had directed in 1961.

Maclean, as we know, was an accomplished Highland dancer, a very different discipline, but immediately saw the potential for groups of country dancers on his Esplanade. *Caber Feidh* or *Mackenzie of Seaforth*, which featured in the Highland Lassies' display, was traced back to the seventeenth century. At first it was performed by men only with the steps and figures designed to portray the loyalty of the Mackenzies. The first figure of the dance signified the hand of friendship, the second with the hand raised portrayed the antlers of the stag, and the third, with the stamp of the feet, symbolised the determination of the Clan. The fourth figure represented the meeting of friends, and the last steps, with the faster music, signified triumph. Another dance in the team's repertoire was *Maclaine of Lochbuie*, an ancient dance revived in the eighteenth century. From then on, Scottish country dancing was to become a popular and innovative feature of the Edinburgh Tattoo.

Fresh from international displays in Berlin, Copenhagen and Milan in 1966 came the Royal Artillery Motor Cycle Display Team. Successor to a small regimental display unit formed by enthusiastic instructors and students of the Royal Artillery Drivers Training Regiment at Rhyl, by 1961 these twenty-four fearless volunteers had gained a considerable reputation for producing displays of considerable skill and daring. In white overalls and silver helmets they soon became a familiar sight at shows and displays throughout the United Kingdom.

However, normally speeds of up to fifty miles per hour were involved, but most of the arenas in which they performed were almost four times the size of the Esplanade. For Edinburgh, therefore, they were obliged to reduce their speed, but all the same included breathtaking formation riding and individual feats of skill. Light relief was provided by two clowns and 'Looney', an antiquated, perverse, but intelligent motor cycle and side car.

A display of gymnastics under Lieutenant Colonel J.W. Gay was given by the Army Physical Training Corps whose primary purpose in the scheme of things was to create and maintain the necessary high

7.2 Costume dramas became a popular feature

standard of fighting fitness and morale required in a modern army. At their headquarters in Aldershot, selected NCOs from all regiments and corps were specifically trained to provide units at home and abroad with instructors capable of teaching physical and recreational training. Instructors were selected from all arms of the Service. Before transferring to the Corps they were required to serve in a unit in the normal way. Only after considerable unit experience were they selected to undergo a further six months intensive training at Aldershot before they were finally accepted as Corps instructors.

The team performing were selected Army Physical Training Corps instructors who were serving either in the United Kingdom or Germany. Their programme consisted of ground gymnastics and trampolining, and with the team were some of the UK's top ranking gymnasts. CMSI Pancott, the reigning British champion, had represented Britain in the 1960 Rome Olympics, the 1964 Tokyo Olympics and the 1965 European Championships. SSI Dooley had represented Britain in many international competitions, SI Wilson had been runner-up in the 1965 World Tumbling Championships, and SSI

Munn had represented the Army in the National Team Championships. On the trampoline was seen CMSI Ions, one time British and Belgian Champion, and assisting him, CMSI Bartlett, Army Boxing Coach, and SI Daley, runner up in the previous year's Army championships. Following this, a demonstration of precision drill was provided by The Queen's Colour Squadron of the Royal Air Force, formerly the Recruits Advanced Drill Unit and the

7.3 Tom Fleming

Ceremonial Drill Unit of the Royal Air Force Regiment, based at Royal Air Force Uxbridge and who represented the Royal Air Force on Royal and National occasions. Included were personnel who had seen active service in Cyprus (The Green Line, Nicosia), Aden (The Radfan operations) and Malaysia (Borneo).

Since 1950, a number of personalities had been responsible for the Tattoo commentaries, from the box and increasingly on television screens. These had included Richard Dimbleby and Raymond Baxter, but by 1966 a gifted actor had emerged gaining enormous respect with his smooth, rich voice. His name was Tom Fleming, and in the years that followed he was to encapsulate the spirit of this great show for a worldwide television audience.

But in many ways the closing night of 1966 was a watershed, because it marked the retirement of the Brigadier. At the time, the then G.O.C. Scotland, Lieutenant General Sir George Gordon Lennox, observed, 'The Tattoo is his creation and his alone'. In retrospect this sounds a trifle unfair to George Malcolm, but it had certainly been Maclean's achievement to elevate Tattoo performances to a world class status.

An often impatient and eccentric individual, those who worked with him found him either exasperating or inspirational, sometimes both, but he was never boring. On one occasion, at a luncheon, an English major passed a derogatory remark about 'Maclean's Threepenny Opera', and this had incensed him. Returning to his office incandescent, he had demanded a set of bagpipes. As soon as they arrived, he set off to General Staff Offices where he knew the officer in question would be working, and proceeded to march up and down the corridor outside the unfortunate man's door playing *Scotland The Brave*.

What usually impressed people most was his sheer professionalism and dedication. He had many small foibles, among them a love of quirky notices which he hung all over the walls of his office. One on the outer door read, 'We have your warmth at heart. Please co-operate by keeping the door shut.' Above his desk he hung a sign which read, 'Certainly we can help you out . . . How did you come in?' Another read, 'Don't do it today. Do it tomorrow. You've made enough mistakes today.'

7.4 RAF police dogs give a display

Alasdair Maclean did know what he was talking about and for him the Tattoo audience came first and the show had always to go on. Philip Gilmore, on duty at the time, recalled one particularly dreich and soaking night when the officer in charge at the Castle, who shall forever remain nameless, had taken it upon himself to cancel a performance because of the bad weather. Driving up Edinburgh's High Street in his car, the Brigadier was astonished to find a large crowd dispersing from the Esplanade and demanded to know what was going on.

'The show's been cancelled,' he was told.

'Absolutely not,' he roared. 'I am in charge. The show will go on!'

It did.

Brigadier Alasdair Maclean died in 1973.

# 8    A Hard Act to Follow

ALASDAIR Maclean's successor clearly needed to be somebody of substance and ability, and once again the right candidate was at hand. The man chosen was a former Scots Guards officer, Brigadier (Retired) Jack Sanderson. He had previously been Maclean's assistant for five years, so it could be said that he hit the ground running.

Jack Sanderson was born in Melbourne, Australia in 1909, and having joined The Scots Guards, proceeded to carve out a distinguished military career during World War Two in Italy and Norway. His postings after that included Palestine and Malaya, and he later served as British Liaison Officer to the American Army at Fort Leavenworth, Kansas, before joining the British contingent at European Forces Headquarters in Fontainbleau, France. Towards the end of his army career he was promoted to Brigadier, Highland District, then Commander, Edinburgh Area.

A jovial character and a noted jazz lover, it was to be expected that the musical content of the Tattoo would broaden, and to this end Major James Howe of The Scots Guards, musical director of the Massed Bands, was once again encouraged to feature his own composition *Robbie Burns on the March*. For the first time in 1968 a vocalist was introduced, Sergeant Muir, a cook from the Scots Guards' Sergeant's Mess, who belted out *If I Ruled the World* and *Land of Hope and Glory*, which Jack always referred to afterwards as 'Land of Hope and Crosby', paying tribute to the American crooner Bing Crosby.

8.1 Brigadier Jack Sanderson

In many ways, however, Sanderson was Maclean's protégé, carrying on a mix of the most up-to-date feats of military skill and strength with memorable historic pageants, a formula which has worked remarkably well to this day.

Nineteen sixty-six being the fiftieth Anniversary of the Royal Society for the Prevention of Accidents, the Royal Navy (all Fleet Air Arm ratings), the Royal Marines, and the Women's Royal Naval Service collaborated in a Vehicle Handling Competition, which had previously been undertaken at the Royal Tournament on an Inter-Service basis. At Edinburgh, however, the competition was between the Royal Navy and the Royal Marines, with members of the WRNS taking part in each team.

The competition was in two parts. First, the WRNS in Minis (saloon cars, not skirts) drove backwards and forwards through a tortuous course between obstacles. The cars were in competition and the faster driver who knocked down the least number of obstacles gained the highest points.

The next part of the test was a men's team event. The Royal Navy and Royal Marines each produced a team of six soldiers with a Land Rover and trailer, who undertook a series of driving problems under simulated operational conditions with explosions, machine-gun fire and breakdowns to create an atmosphere of violence and urgency. The team which successfully surmounted all obstacles won the event, the points gained by the two teams (Mini and Land Rover) added together for the final score.

Another splendid spectacle was a parade of military horses through the ages, with historical figures enacted by local recruits. Second Lieutenant J. Scott-Barrett of the 15th/19th The King Royal Hussars was the Officer in Charge.

The overseas input was equally colourful. The origins of the Jamaica Regiment dated back to 1795 when the Malcolms Corps of Rangers was raised, later to be redesignated the 1st West India Regiment. By 1799 the number of West India regiments had risen to twelve, and were used to garrison Britain's Carribean Colonies. In

1812, the 2nd West India Regiment moved to Sierra Leone and fought in the first Ashanti War of 1824. The 1st and 2nd were disbanded in 1927, but on the formation of the Federation of the West Indies it was decided to re-raise them and the 1st Battalion was reformed in Jamaica in 1959. When Jamaica opted out of the Federation in 1961, the West India Regiment was again disbanded and the Jamaica Defence Force raised in its place. Tattoo audiences were thus privileged to hear the Band of the 1st Battalion stationed in Kingston, and to witness a display of folk dancing and singing from the 3rd (National Reserve) Battalion, trained on a part-time basis and coming up with such evergreen favourites as *Yellow Bird*.

On top of this, a musical and physical training display was given by the Italian army featuring the Fanfara and the physical training team of the 8th Regiment Bersaglieri. This Corps was raised in Turin

8.2  La Fanfara dei Bersaglieri

in 1836 by Captain Alessandro La Marmora, who had wanted to establish a new type of mobile light infantry, armed with modern carbines.

The meaning of the name 'Bersaglieri' is 'Soldiers who hit the target (*bersaglio*)', in other words, 'sharp-shooters', but ironically, it was through their involvement with the Tattoo that Jack Sanderson would have to face up to the Tattoo's first financial crisis.

Fully pledged and accounted for separately from the Edinburgh Festival Society, the Edinburgh Military Tattoo had forged ahead financially throughout the 1950s, in every way a remarkable achievement. In succeeding years, surplus had followed surplus, and by the end of the decade these had amounted in total to £177,941. Of this amount, service charities benefited to the extent of £82,275, whilst the Festival Society received £107,274. The Reserve Fund stood at £19,517.

The same pattern continued into the early 1960s, but by the middle of that decade the size of the surplus began to diminish and withdrawals had to be made from the Reserve Fund to maintain the same level of distribution to charities as in previous years.

This change in the fortunes of the Tattoo was obviously attributable to increased expenditure while ticket prices remained at the same level as in previous years. In short, budgetary control was not being properly or consistently exercised, and the cracks were beginning to show. By 1968, the withdrawals from the Reserve Fund had left only £2,011 in credit, and it just needed a slight push for the Tattoo Committee to have a larger problem on its hands.

The push, innocent enough, and entirely unintentional, came from the Italian Bersaglieri. The Fanfara and 8th Regiment had been invited to take part in the Tattoo, and an offer from the Italian Air Force to provide air transport from Italy to Edinburgh and back at the conclusion of the Tattoo had been accepted by the organisers as preferable to the costs involved with charter flights. The arrangement appeared admirable, but things began to go wrong from the start.

8.3 The Drums

To begin with, it had not been taken into account that the Italian transport planes would need to refuel en route to Scotland, and this dramatically increased the cost of their travel. Then it transpired they would be landing at Prestwick Airport instead of at Edinburgh's Turnhouse Airport, where a welcoming party had already assembled.

It was late at night, and after hurried calls to the Junior Training Regiment at Troon, the Bersaglieri were accomodated for the night and transported to Edinburgh on the following day. Thereafter everything went well enough, so it seemed. The Bersaglieri's contribution to the Tattoo was pronounced a dazzling success, but then a few weeks later an invoice arrived from the Italian Air Force for the fuel consumed in the venture, a significant sum.

Although the Tattoo had prospered up to that point on a somewhat informal basis, it was now clear that a more stringent financial control needed to be imposed by the participating principals, Edinburgh Corporation and the Army, and a Tattoo Policy Committee was hurriedly established, on the basis of an annual agreement by both parties. This consisted of three officers and a civilian from the Army, namely the Brigadier Lowlands, the Senior Staff Officer, the Paymaster from HQ Scotland, and the District Secretary. The City was represented by the City Treasurer, two other elected members and the City Chamberlain, and they were joined by the Tattoo's Producer and its Business Manager.

From its inauguration the Tattoo Policy Committee set out to establish close control of its officials' activities through regular meetings and a system of budgetary control which, particularly in the early years of its work, involved strict limitation of expenditure and close scrutiny of income, especially a regular review of ticket prices to restore the firm foundation for the Tattoo's future productions. At that time it was agreed that the financial target for the Reserve Fund should be set at £100,000, and under the new regime profitability on a regular basis was rapidly restored.

However, there were other problems to be addressed. The result of a Government Defence Review in 1967 was that the Infantry Regiments of the Army were regrouped, and cuts made. In Scotland, it meant the loss of The Cameronians (Scottish Rifles), whose disbandment in May 1968 brought to an end 279 years of distinguished service to the Crown.

# 9   Comings and Goings

IN 1968, the seven surviving Scottish infantry regiments – The Royal Scots (The Royal Regiment), The Royal Highland Fusiliers (Princess Margaret's Own Glasgow and Ayrshire Regiment), The King's Own Scottish Borderers, The Black Watch, The Queen's Own Highlanders, The Gordon Highlanders, and The Argyll and Sutherland Highlanders – assembled together to form one family of regiments within the British Army. Scottish Division, an administrative grouping was created to take the place of the former Highland and Lowland brigades.

At the Tattoo they were joined in a display of pipes and drums and Highland dancing by The Royal Scots Greys (2nd Dragoons), Scotland's senior regiment and only regiment of cavalry. Also performing were The Regimental Band, 2nd Gurkhas, Pipes and Drums selected from the 6th, 7th and 10th Gurkha Rifles, the Engineers and Signals, and the Kukuri Display Team from the 2nd Gurkhas. Tribute was paid to the fiftieth Anniversary of the formation of the Royal Air Force, with massed bands comprising the Band of The Royal Corps of Transport, The Royal Air Force Regiment, and the Band and Choir of the 1st Battalion, The Welch Regiment.

The Welch Regiment had been in existence for 250 years, having been raised in 1719 as a Regiment of Invalids, out-pensioners from the Royal Hospital Chelsea, for garrison duties in the United Kingdom. This was later to give rise to the nickname 'Invalids' when it became a field marching regiment known as the 41st Foot in 1787.

Oddly enough, there was no connection with South Wales at all until forty-four years later when it was designated the 41st Foot The Welch Regiment.

The 69th Foot, raised in 1756, spent most of its early years at sea, acting as Marines in the Fleet, and notably providing a detachment in Lord Nelson's flagship. Amalgamating with the 41st Foot in 1881 to become respectively the 1st and 2nd Battalion, The Welch Regiment, and thereafter its soldiers, fought in the South African War, raised thirty-four Battalions in World War One and during World War Two fought in Crete, the Western Desert, Sicily, Italy and Burma.

From New Brunswick in the State of New Jersey, USA came The Queens Guard, Rutgers University, cadets from a Reserve Officers Training Corps (ROTC) formed in 1919. In 1933, the Scarlet Rifles was formed at Rutgers University as a drill team completely separate from ROTC, but was eventually incorporated into the Army ROTC

9.1 The Queens Guard, Rutgers University – one of the top drill teams in the USA

unit. During the 1952-53 school year, an Air Force Scarlet Rifles team was formed and in 1957 changed its name to The Queens Guard, after Queen's College, Rutger's original name, in order to achieve complete autonomy. As Tattoo visitors were to witness for themselves, it had since established itself as one of the top drill teams in the USA.

A 'skilled driving competition' was proposed and sub-units throughout Scotland, Regular and Territorial, were encouraged to enter four-man teams. Colonel Robert S.B. Watson of The Royal Scots, at the time a junior officer and Adjutant to Lieutenant Colonel David Ward of the KOSB at the then Lowland Brigade Depot at Glencorse, was encouraged to take part.

'In a fit of enthusiasm, David Ward said to enter four teams in the belief that there would be so many entrants that we would probably only get one or two places,' explained Watson.

They were allocated all four, but undeterred Ward immediately issued a personal challenge to Lieutenant Colonel Andy Watson, then commanding 1st Battalion, The Black Watch at Kirknewton Barracks, to meet him on the Esplanade at the appointed hour with their respective adjutants, regimental sergeant majors, and chief clerks.

'I suspect that with two lieutenant colonels, two captains, two warrant officers class 1, and two warrant officers class 2, these were probably the two most senior teams ever to participate in the Tattoo,' admitted Robert Watson .

History records that the depot won narrowly, the major hazard, apart from the appalling driving of the two lieutenant colonels, being a somewhat unpleasant contribution left behind on the Esplanade by a Welch Regiment goat participating with their bands in a previous item.

Nineteen sixty-eight was the year in which the full spectacle of the Tattoo was first captured on television screens in glorious colour. The effect was twofold, for although it meant that viewers could now enjoy the Tattoo in all its splendour from the comfort of their own homes anywhere in the world, it made others all the more determined to travel to Scotland for a first-hand experience. It also enhanced the glamour of the occasion. Between 1966 and 1969, the GOC Scotland, Lieutenant General Sir Derek Lang, found himself entertaining in the Royal Box the French film star Maurice Chevalier, the journalist Malcolm Muggeridge, the comedy star Bebe Daniels, the war hero Douglas Bader, and the Duke of Norfolk. Representing the Royal Family, the Duke and Duchess of Kent and Princess Alexandra came too.

The British Columbia Beefeater Band from Canada had officially represented its province and country at three World Fairs in North America, namely Seattle, New York, and Montreal. Three years previously this band had been officially presented at the Tournament of Roses in California, as part of the British Columbian Contingent, and the following year had played a feature role in the opening ceremonies of the Pan-American Games in Winnipeg. Scarlet and black, their uniforms were an authentic copy of those worn by the celebrated Beefeaters who guard the Tower of London, and the applause for these young musicians ranging in age from between seventeen and twenty, from an audience now representative of all the continents of the world, was tumultuous.

One of the best known characters from this period was Brigadier 'Jock' Balharrie, who served on the Tattoo Committee from 1969 until 1972. Every evening Jock would appear resplendent in the full dress uniform of his beloved Scots Greys. For those unfamiliar with Scotland's premier cavalry regiment, the dress uniform of the Scots Greys comprises chain mail epaulettes, stripes on the trousers, gleaming boots and in the Brigadier's case, it was rumoured, solid gold spurs that fitted into the heel of each boot.

However, during one performance it was discovered that Jock was missing a spur, and for an officer of his standing this was equivalent to being naked. The word went around and a frantic search took place, but no spur was found. It was, of course, a sign of the respect in which he was held that after the performance large numbers of the cast volunteered to stay on and conduct a line search until the missing spur was found. And found it was.

Reporting on this afterwards, journalist Ben-Aryeah recorded: 'That night all the troops got a drink – on Jock!'

For the 1970 performances, the Scottish Division was once more out in force, joined by The Royal Leicestershire Regiment, which in its history as the 17th Regiment of Foot had garrisoned Edinburgh Castle in 1714 under its Constable and Governor, Lord George Hamilton, Captain of Foot.

Also taking part was The Blues and Royals (Royal Horse Guards and 1st Dragoons), which as part of the reorganisation of the British Army had been formed on 29th March with the amalgamation of The Royal Horse Guards (The Blues) and the Royal Dragoons (1st Dragoons). In company with The Life Guards, it now formed The Household Cavalry, the senior corps in the British Army, a marriage between two of Britain's finest.

The Blues traced their origins back to the regiment of horse, raised by parliament in 1650 prior to Oliver Cromwell's second invasion of Scotland. In common with the rest of the Army, the regiment was disbanded in 1650, but was re-raised in 1661 as The Royal Regiment of Horse.

For their part, the Royal Dragoons were raised by Charles II in 1661 to garrison Tangier, which had become a British territory with his marriage to Catherine of Braganza. In 1683, the regiment returned to England and subsequently served in the major European campaigns of the eighteenth century, as indeed did The Blues, sharing many of the battle honours of this period. The Royals also charged with the Heavy Brigade at Balaclava, and both regiments served with distinction during World War Two. Since then, both had been serving in various theatres, namely Egypt, Aden, Malaya, Singapore, Cyprus and with the British Army of the Rhine.

The Sultan of Brunei himself came to Edinburgh to take the salute when officers and men and the regimental band of the Royal Brunei Malay Police enacted a ceremonial and historical display. Formed in 1961, this regiment was originally a three hundred strong ceremonial force, but quickly expanded into an infantry battalion as a result of the revolt in Brunei, taking part in the Indonesian confrontation in the Brunei area in 1964.

At the end of the run of 1970, T.K. Currie retired as Tattoo Business Manager and Alex Thain, his assistant of three years, took over. After twenty years, T.K.'s departure was not to be taken lightly. Lieutenant Colonel Bobby Smith, Secretary of the Tattoo Committee in 1962, especially remembered him presiding over working lunches in the North British Hotel (now the Balmoral Hotel). 'They were memorable meetings, not at all stuffy, and rarely ended before five,' he said. 'Believe it or not we achieved an enormous amount at them.'

But with Alex Thain, the Tattoo was in safe hands for the next eight years. A former employee of Edinburgh Corporation, he had the added accomplishment of having once been a bandmaster with the Salvation Army.

With the exception of the return of the Brigade of Ghurkhas, the 1971 Tattoo was entirely home grown with The Royal Scots Dragoon Guards, The Scottish Division, The Royal Artillery, The Royal Air Force Regiment and The Sea Cadet Corps presenting a lively programme.

However, it was during a Force 8 gale one night that the voice of the Tattoo Producer could be heard shouting over the public address system, and above the sound of the Pipes and Drums, 'Will Mr Laing please attend to the microphone on the top of the South Stand as it appears to be moving.' Moving was an understatement, according to Bryce Laing, who was involved with the sound recording. 'The microphone and mounting had almost blown over. A colleague and I battled up as fast as we could and managed to secure it by us both lying face down on the catwalk boards and holding on to the stand until the end of the performance.'

The Royal Norwegian Guard (HM Kongens Garde) were back in 1972, with The Scottish Division, The Life Guards, and The Coldstream Guards, but the highlight was undoubtedly provided by members of the Singapore People's Defence Force who gave a display of sword drill followed by the colourful Frog Dance supervised by

Major Eng Song King, Sergeant Yip Peng Kee, and WO II Chia Shue Foy.

From overseas also came The Pipes and Drums of The Scots College (Sydney), Australia and, for a second visit, The Queens Guard, Rutgers University, USA

The Scots College Pipe Band, which took part in the finale, was formed in 1900 and was the oldest pipe band in New South Wales. For sixty years the numbers within the band had remained relatively small, but since 1960, under the direction and leadership of Captain Ronald Murray, had increased in membership to 150 pipers and drummers, in various stages of training. Of interest to some, perhaps, was the fact that one of the bass drums being played on the Esplanade had the signature on its skin of Field Marshal Lord

9.2 Royal Navy display, 1971

Montgomery of Alamein, who had appended his signature while inspecting the band in 1947.

Joining the show also that year were personnel from the Royal Navy in Scotland from Rosyth Dockyard in the Firth of Forth, and bases on the River Clyde and River Tay, and for the first time men and women from Edinburgh and Heriot-Watt Universities Officers Training Corps took part in the displays of Scottish dancing.

Having featured in the Tattoo of 1963, the South Eastern Fire Brigade, as the oldest municipal fire brigade in the United Kingdon, were back to illustrate 150 years of fire fighting. There was also The Sri Lankan Police Reserve established in 1949 to serve as an auxiliary to the Regular Police Service, and which was completely reorganised

9.3 The War Drums of Sri Lanka, 1973

in 1971. The Reserve's Hewisi Band, formed the following year, consisted of volunteers highly skilled in the indigenous forms of drumming and dancing.

It was the year of Major James Howe's retirement from the army after 41 years of service and when the Massed Bands gathered together for their triumphal climax, Jack Sanderson insisted that *Wish Me Luck As You Wave Me Goodbye* be played as he marched around the arena.

Sir Chandos Blair, who was GOC Scotland between 1972 until 1976, was a great admirer of the Royal Air Force Gymnastic Display Team, based at St Albans, but when he had first suggested they be invited to perform, he was told they had declined because the slope of the Esplanade was too steep. However, shortly after this, Air-Vice Marshal Pete Williamson, a great friend, took over AOC Training Command, and Sir Chandos made a point of inviting him and his wife to come and stay for a couple of days during the 1973 Edinburgh Festival.

The result, of course, was that the following year the RAF were only too delighted to put together a gymnastic and physical training display with RAF and WRAF personnel. An interesting footnote is that the RAF School of Physical Training was one of the oldest training schools in the RAF with a history dating back to 1918 when one of the first officers – and its tennis coach – was Prince Albert, later to become King George VI.

During the early 1970s, surpluses in the Tattoo accounts had on average exceeded £20,000, and despite a small deficit in 1974 (£3,861), they continued to increase over the following three years, a time when the pound was weak on international money markets, a circumstance which attracted many overseas visitors to Scotland and, of course, to the Tattoo.

However, it was during this period that two events occurred which temporarily removed the Tattoo's organisation from the regular smooth progress it had enjoyed hitherto. These were the Reorganisation of Local Government in Scotland in 1975 and, a year earlier, an event which caused the Tattoo Policy Committee to change the method of erecting its spectator stands.

9.4 (*overleaf*) The 1974 Finale

Of these two events, the story of the stands is covered in a later chapter. As for Local Government Reorganisation, a Royal Commission, chaired by Lord Wheatley, a Scottish judge, had been established in the late 1960s, and now recommended the setting up of a two-tier system of local government on mainland Scotland. This had been accepted by central Government.

The effect of these changes, so far as they concerned the Tattoo, was that on 16th May 1975, Edinburgh Corporation ceased to exist and was replaced by two local authorities, Lothian Regional Council and the City of Edinburgh District Council. The latter became responsible for 'recreation services', and it was therefore the City of Edinburgh District Council which the Tattoo Policy Committee were required to approach for the support previously provided by Edinburgh Corporation. Happily, the District Council readily agreed, and the General Officer Commanding Scotland gave an assurance that military support for the Tattoo would continue as before, under the new local government arrangements.

Over his period as General Officer Commanding the Army in Scotland, Sir Chandos and Lady Blair regularly invited friends with children to stay at Gogarbank House, taking them as their guests to the Royal Box. At breakfast on the following morning, Sir Chandos would interrogate the children about the Tattoo to find out what they had enjoyed best. Invariably it was the official car ride with the police escort, jumping red lights as they went until they arrived on the Castle Esplanade, but there was one exception. This was a seven-year old girl who had arrived at Gogarbank mid-afternoon with her mother, and since they needed entertaining, the General had taken them to the zoo on Corstorphine Hill.

'I hadn't been to Edinburgh Zoo since 1930 and was interested to see if there was still a notice on display in the Elephant House which read "Beware of the Elephant's Posterior",' he recalled with a chuckle. 'When I asked the little girl the usual question about the Tattoo at breakfast the next day, she replied that she had liked the okapi best because he got into the water to do his biggies!'

9.5  Maori dancers, 1975

'So much for the expensive smash hits at the Tattoo!' said the
General.

After the last performance of 1975, Jack Sanderson retired and
took on the job of chairman of The British Limbless Ex-Servicemen's
Association Home in Crieff. He died at the age of seventy-five in
1985.

# 10   The Voice of the Castle

THERE now followed an important period in the Tattoo's continued development under the nurturing of yet another remarkable character, Lieutenant-Colonel Leslie Dow, who became Producer in 1976 and continued in the role for fifteen years. Under his innovative control, what was already established as a magnificent military pageant began to be recognised as one of the most impressive military entertainments on offer anywhere in the world.

Leslie Phillips Graham Dow was born in Glasgow in 1926 and educated at Marlborough College in England. He enlisted in the Army in 1944, was commissioned into The Cameronians (Scottish Rifles) in 1945, and thereafter served in Gibraltar, Trieste, Hong Kong, Malaya and Germany. In 1961, he became a company commander at Sandhurst, and three years later was appointed military assistant to General Freeland, GOC, East Africa.

Next an appointment in the military secretary's office at the War Office found him working on a study of the Officer Confidential Reporting System where he became noted for making such acute observations as 'He is a good man in a crisis, which is just as well as his presence would probably cause one.'

In 1965 Leslie Dow attended the Joint Services Staff College at Latimer, and the following year assumed command of 1st Battalion, The Cameronians (Scottish Rifles) for the Aden Campaign, where the regiment acquitted itself with distinction, perhaps with too much distinction because it returned to discover that it was to be disbanded in the latest round of National Defence Expenditure cuts of 1968.

10.1 Lieutenant Colonel Leslie Dow

What was even more ironic is that the official date set for this dispersal was exactly 279 years to the day that the regiment had been raised by the Earl of Angus. Determined that it should be an occasion never to be forgotten by those who were present at it, Dow undertook to supervise personally the ceremony on the very same site as the original fighting men had first been assembled at Douglas Dale in Lanarkshire.

And as was to be expected, for the men and their families, many of whom had been associated with the regiment for generations, it was a profoundly moving occasion. Dow had done them and the regiment proud, but afterwards, having been transferred to the King's Own Scottish Borderers, he decided to leave the military.

Shortly before doing so, he received his OBE insignia from The Queen at Buckingham Palace and insisted on wearing the Douglas tartan trews and the leather cross belts of his old regiment.

'You're wearing the wrong uniform,' observed the sharp-eyed monarch.

'But this is the one I won the award in ma'am,' he replied.

A short stint in industry working for his father-in-law filled the gap, but before long he was persuaded to apply for the Edinburgh Military Tattoo post of producer which had become vacant. Not least among those who cajoled him into it was Tom Fleming who had not only provided the television commentary for the Cameronian's disbandment parade, but whose rich voice had by then already become an established feature from the commentary box at the Tattoo.

It was Leslie Dow who introduced 'The Voice of the Castle', a soliloquy in which the mighty fortress welcomed its visitors, reflected upon its turbulent history and affirmed its continuing role as guardian of the Scottish Capital. Corny though it might be considered nowadays, it struck a chord. The aged, solid fortification on its rock which had seen the centuries come and go fuelled the imagination with feats of daring, bravery, romance and treachery witnessed first hand.

And daring and bravery were also qualities embodied in the personality of this latest Producer of the Edinburgh Military Tattoo. Writing on Dow's first Tattoo for a subsequent souvenir brochure, Nicholas Radcliffe, the former television journalist, recorded the following scene:

> Imagine a mild evening in late summer. A troop of powerful motorcycles forms up just inside the Castle drawbridge, the sound of their engines reverberating like drumfire on the walls. As the gates open and the motorbikes roar onto the esplanade, 9,000 spectators thrill with anticipation – and one thrills with horror, for marching with the motorcycles is a man who calmly lies on the tarmac and allows the riders to hurl their machines over him in a series of daring leaps and stunts. The horrified woman in the audience was Mrs Dow. And the supine volunteer beneath the whizzing wheels was her husband, the Producer.

With Leslie Dow's arrival in 1976 there was also a new incumbent at Gogarbank House, with Lieutenant-General Sir David Scott-Barrett taking over from Sir Chandos Blair as General Officer Commanding Scotland and Governor of Edinburgh Castle.

From Italy came the The Banda dell' Arma dei Carabinieri under the direction of Maestro Vincenzo Borgia. Founded in 1885 when the trumpeters of the 24th Carabinieri were transferred from Turin, the birthplace of the Corps, to Rome, the capital of the newly-created State of Italy, the band had become world famous. Maestro Borgia had been appointed in 1972 and the band's repertoire extended from traditional Italian military music to the music of the well-known composers, both classical and contemporary.

'As a gesture of our growing friendship, a lunch was arranged at one of the local Italian restaurants,' recorded Major, later Lieutenant Colonel, Stanley Patch, Director of Music of The Royal Engineers Band, Aldershot. 'On arrival we were shown to our table by a very disinterested staff, who then seemed to ignore us completely. Our conversation was beginning to become a little strained, all my musical

10.2 Italy's Banda dell' Arma dei Carabinieri

Italian terms being long exhausted, and Vincenzo was becoming as impatient as my wife and I. Ten minutes of being ignored by the staff had passed when he pushed back his chair, drew himself up to his full five feet five inches and made his way across to the wayward waiters whereupon he proceeded to address them in a torrent of Italian. On his return to the table, needless to say, the service was magnificent. Waiters hovered on our every whim. The food was delicious; the wine, excellent. In every way it was a gastronomic delight.'

The Berlin Brigade Drill Team of the United States Army was another hit. Dating from 1972 its members were drawn from all three battalions of 6th US Infantry, and they had been performing at American and German events, at Honour Ceremonies and other functions, throughout West Berlin, the Federal Republic of Germany and Belgium. The Drill Team's precision drill consisted of a series of difficult and complex manoeuvres which involved the handling of a 9-pound rifle fitted with a razor-sharp bayonet. The drill is entirely committed to memory and one error could lead to serious injury.

At the same time a greater freedom was beginning to be enjoyed between visiting Tattoo performers and the city at large. Festival artistes regularly turned up as spectators at the Castle, and soldiers from military units began to find time to disperse after hours in search of what Scotland's Capital had to offer in the way of night life. In those days this very much centred upon the Fringe Club, quartered at the University's McEwen Hall or the Festival Club, located in the Assembly Rooms in George Street.

The Monday before the Dresden State Orchestra was scheduled to play in the Usher Hall, Lord Provost Kenneth Borthwick was hosting a supper party in the east drawing room of the Festival Club when George Bain, the Festival's organising secretary, came up to him and whispered, 'We have a problem, Lord Provost. The members of the Dresden State Orchestra have just arrived at Edinburgh Airport and apparently it is too late for them to have a meal.'

It was around 11.30pm, so the Lord Provost agreed that two buses should be sent immediately to the airport to bring them to the Festival Club where a meal was prepared for them. In the meantime, Bain suggested it might make the German performers feel more welcome if the Lord Provost received them personally.

'What shall I say to them?' he asked Bain.

'Just welcome them to Edinburgh,' he replied. 'Ich bin der Oberbürgermeister von Edinbourg, wilkommen!'

Doing his best to memorise the words, Lord Provost Borthwick moved from table to table in an attempt to make the ravenous Germans feel at home. Finally, when he reached the eighth table and was about to say his piece, one of the group jumped up and said: 'Och dinnae worry about us, Lord Provost. We're just pipers in The Argyll and Sutherland Highlanders.' Hearing that food was being served to Festival guests at the Festival Club, they had slipped in to see what was on offer. Both the Lord Provost and the Festival Secretary burst out laughing.

Nineteen seventy-seven was the year of HM The Queen's Silver Jubilee celebrations, and with The Queen's Silver Jubilee in mind, The Royal Regiment of Wales, The Worcester and Sherwood Foresters Regiment, The Royal Irish Rangers, and The Argyll and

Sutherland Highlanders had sent their mascots, a tremendous success with the younger members of the audience.

Soldiers have always kept pets, usually dogs of indeterminate ancestry, many of which went into battle with their owners in the more spacious days of combat. The original goat of The Welsh Regiment took part in the Crimean War, and Taffy II, the goat of The Royal Regiment of Wales, had been taken on strength in 1974 on the death of his predecessor. His official name was Gwilym Jenkins and on this occasion he was led onto the parade ground by Goat-Major Baggett.

According to records, the original ram mascot of The Sherwood Foresters had been 'acquired' during the Indian Mutiny and survived six battles. On this occasion, Derby XIII, a Swaledale ram, wore the Indian Mutiny and General Service medals awarded to two of his distinguished predecessors in the charge of Ram-Major Crump and Ram-Orderly Fish. This was Derby's first big parade, and by all accounts he conducted himself with great dignity.

10.3 Brian Boru VI, mascot of the band of The Royal Irish Rangers

Brian Boru II had been purchased by The Royal Irish Rangers in 1976 to replace the first wolfhound mascot of the regiment, discharged that same year on pension to live on a farm in County Wexford. This Brian Boru was born in County Mayo in 1976 and under his handler Corporal Devine 'passed off the square' with the new squad of recruits on St Patrick's Day.

Finally, Cruachan II, bred at Braes of Greenoch, near Callander, in Perthshire, had joined the Argylls in 1952, making his debut at the Tattoo the following year. He had served in Germany and Cyprus, and was looked after by Pony-Major Denholm, a former apprentice jockey who was on parade when new colours were presented to The Argyll and Sutherland Highlanders by HM the Queen in 1953 and 1973.

10.4 'Does the queue start here?' Cruachan, mascot of The Argyll and Sutherland Highlanders, outside the ticket office

To the delight of the crowds, marines of the 45 Commando, Royal Marines, from Arbroath, in north-east Scotland, demonstrated a cliff assault, and there was plenty of precision marching and continuity drilling from The Queen's Colour Squadron of the Royal Air Force, who in the past year, aside from public duties at St James's Palace, Buckingham Palace and The Tower of London, had provided royal guards of honour for the President of France and the President of Tanzania.

The Auld Alliance, a treaty first forged between Scotland and France in 1295, was commemorated by La Batterie-Fanfare de la Garde Republicaine de Paris, commanded by General de Brigade Personnier. Formed in the year 1254 by King Louis IX of France for the civic peace of Paris, its primary task was still the maintenance of law and order in Paris, but it had also remained part of the French

Army, comprising an infantry regiment of three battalions, a cavalry regiment of four horsed squadrons, and one motor cycle squadron with various supporting technical services

That August, La Batterie-Fanfare was commanded by Adjutant-Chief Tambour Major G. Hebrard, and consisted of seventy-four musicians who formed a military band and corps of drums and 'clairons', the traditional French bugle. The instruments employed differed from those usually found in British bands, producing a distinctively French sound. The programme therefore consisted of a medley of French military music including some of the brilliant marches to which France holds the secret, together with drum and bugle signals dating back to the time of Napoleon. The show concluded with the beautiful *L'extinction des feux (Lights out)* call of the French Army.

10.5 La Garde Republicaine de Paris

# 11   Amazing Grace

IN 1977, the Tattoo team was joined by Major Brian Leishman, late of The Kings Own Scottish Borderers, formerly of The Cameronians (Scottish Rifles). Dundee-born and educated at Fettes College, he was no stranger to Scotland's Capital.

As Assistant Defence Attaché to the British Embassy in Rome, Leishman had been involved in the preparations leading up to the Carabinieri Band's participation in the 1976 Tattoo, and was invited to act as their interpreter when they visited. Another Italian group, provided by the Italian State Tourist Board, comprised a posse of girls and boys who were attending their Tourism School in Italy.

'The nightly vision of the Director of Music Vincenzo Borgia and I embracing in true Italian style under the East Stand after each of the bands had performed was a sight viewed with the gravest suspicion by the Royal Military Police and no doubt others,' said Leishman with a chuckle. 'They must have thought I had taken leave of my senses. A Scottish upbringing does not prepare one for the tactile approach of the Italian, although I have to say that my experience of this Italian approach was one that I learned to appreciate since my own rather stuffy approach left much to be desired.'

This Italian association was in fact Leishman's third attachment to the Tattoo before becoming a member of staff. In 1962 he had brought a detachment of the Infantry Junior Leaders to the show as a drill display team, and in 1968 had been interpreter for the Italian Bersaglieri Fanfara (band) and Drill Display Team.

11.1 Major Brian Leishman

By the end of 1976, he was thinking long and hard about his future in soldiering and spotted an advertisement for the post of Assistant Business Manager with the Tattoo. He applied and got the job, later discovering that there had been 321 applicants.

To begin with, returning from Italy was something of an anti-climax for him. He remembered setting off from Rome in convoy with two stops en route and arriving in Edinburgh late one cold early evening to collect the keys for his new home close to Redford Barracks. 'My choice to return home rather than seek a posting else-where was motivated by wanting to see my children Robin and Alison settled in UK schools after schools in Germany and Italy,' he said. 'Thereafter, it was a steep learning curve, becoming involved with every aspect of the business.'

Twenty years on, Leishman could proudly boast that there was not one task within the administrative operation that he had not at some stage tackled, from taking telephone calls to selling tickets at the box office counter.

On one occasion, shortly after lunch, a man dived out of a passing car and rushed into the crowded box office screaming out that those present should not support the murdering military by buying tickets for their Tattoo. Another time, a young man was discovered with his hands in an open till after the box office had closed. 'When I asked what he was doing, he replied he was looking for the toilet,' said Leishman. 'When I informed him he was looking in the wrong place, he and his accomplices fled out the door.'

There was seemingly no end to the eccentricities of the general public. When the building was undergoing refurbishment and was surrounded by scaffolding, a man was observed removing a picture frame from the office walls. When challenged he said that he thought the building was being demolished and wanted a souvenir.

Featuring prominently in the 1978 Tattoo were The Royal Scots Dragoon Guards and The Royal Highland Fusiliers, with a memo-rable display to celebrate their common tercentenary. Officers in charge were Major R.H. de R. Channer and Major

11.2 Darth Vader appears on the Esplanade

Melville S. Jameson, Band President, who nineteen years later was to return to the Tattoo as its Producer. It was Jameson, then Band President, and the Royal Scots Dragoon Guards Military Band and Pipes and Drums, who recorded the song 'Amazing Grace', which was performed at the Tattoo that year. This reached number one in the British Pop Hit Parade and remained there for six weeks, and went on to become a huge international success.

'Bringing the bands together was considered sacrilege at the time,' he recalled later. 'However, it heralded a new era in military music – the combination of Pipes and Drums and Military Band was emulated across the world. The idea came from the then Sergeant Tony Crease, now Major Crease MBE BEM. The Pipe Major was Jimmy Pryde and the Bandmaster, who arranged the score, was Bandmaster Stewart Fairbairn.'

The Royal Scots Dragoon Guards and The Royal Highland Fusiliers share a common origin as well as a badge depicting the Scottish Order of the Thistle surrounded by the motto, *'Nemo me impune lacessit'*, which loosely means 'Wha daur meddle wi' me!'

Back in 1678, Charles II had tried to introduce obligatory episcopacy to Scotland, but there had been determined resistance, particularly in Ayrshire, Dumfries and Galloway. To combat this, three independent troops of Dragoons, mounted infantry, were formed, which were eventually absorbed into the British Army as The Royal Regiment of Scots Dragoons and The Scots Fusiliers. The former were later re-named The Royal Scots Greys, after their grey horses, and the latter became The Royal Scots Fusiliers.

With the formation of The Royal Scots Dragoon Guards' first official pipe band in 1946, its pipers were granted permission by King George VI to wear Royal Stewart tartan. Pipers of The Royal Highland Fusiliers wore the Dress Erskine tartan of their founder, the Earl of Mar, which had been granted to them by King George V in 1928 to commemorate the regiment's two hundred and fiftieth anniversary.

Furthermore, both regiments had more intimate Royal connections, the Queen being colonel-in-chief of the Royal Scots Dragoon Guards in which the Duke of Kent had until recently been a serving officer. Princess Margaret, Countess of Snowdon, was colonel-in-chief of The Royal Highland Fusiliers.

To celebrate a long tradition of 'ridings' in the Scottish Borders, the closing spectacle of the 1978 Tattoo re-enacted a ceremony associated with the annual Selkirk Common Riding known as *Casting the Colour*. Featuring a group of actors and the Massed Military Bands, a programme of music was specially prepared by the well-known Scottish musician and composer Professor Cedric Thorpe Davie.

The rituals of the Selkirk Common Riding are believed to have originated after the Battle of Flodden. The tradition goes that in 1513 eighty men set forth from the town to fight the English and only one returned, one of five brothers called Fletcher. Safely home in the Market Place, he stopped, raised a blood-stained English banner, and cast it in grief to the ground. In that gesture, the folk of Selkirk learned that all but one of her youngest and bravest had died with their king on Flodden Field.

Guests from abroad that year were the Bands of the Royal Hong Kong Police Force, and the Locheil Marching Team, a troop of strikingly attractive girls from the City of Wellington in New Zealand.

During the First World War, both the Chinese and Portuguese companies of the Hong Kong Police Reserve had a pipe band. Afterwards, the Reserve was disbanded, and it was not until the 1950s that a pipe and drum band was formed. Consisting of over one hundred musicians under the company's Director of Music C.C. Wood, formerly Bandmaster of the 1st Battalion Duke of Wellington's Regiment (West Riding), it was interesting to reflect that all of those who were taking part in this occasion were trained police officers, as were those who took part in the indigenous section of the display, the Northern Lions and the dancing.

11.3 The Drum Major, Royal Hong Kong Police Force, 1978

General Sir Michael Gow, who became GOC Scotland in 1979, told the story of how his predecessor, Lieutenant General Sir David Scott-Barrett, invited him to Edinburgh to be briefed on his new command, and in particular to see how he, a 'super enthusiast', handled the Military Tattoo. Indeed, Sir Michael was informed that Sir David had attended every rehearsal and performance, at which point somebody added, 'Yes, and he watched it on television too!'

11.4 The Royal Hong Kong Police Force's magnificent display

It was Sir David's custom to hold large dinner parties every night for the distinguished individuals whom had been invited to take the salute, and to one such occasion was Sir Michael invited.

'We had just assembled in the drawing room of Gogarbank House when suddenly our host darted in dressed as an Arab sheikh,' he recalled. 'We were told to pay close attention. We were informed that we were all really going to enjoy ourselves. All the participants were as enthusiastic as he expected us to be, so we were to give them our full support.

'We were also told that when he had finished talking we should go straight into dinner where we would be told where to sit, and that we had exactly twenty-five minutes to eat it. When our host blew a whistle it was the signal for us all to go to the cloakroom and we were allocated five minutes. Then we should assemble back in the drawing room to be told about transport.'

Sure enough, precisely twenty-five minutes later there was a piercing blast on a whistle and everybody scampered out to obey the instructions. When they reassembled they found their host wearing a fireman's helmet.

'It made all the dinners we held when I took over seem very dull by comparison,' said Sir Michael.

11.5  The Drum Major, The Royal Scots (The Royal Regiment)

# 12    Never a Dull Moment

ALEX Thain had been business manager of the Tattoo for eight years when he handed it over to Brian Leishman in 1978.

Staffing was, and remains, a vital factor in the success of the operation. A small dedicated team who work well together is essential to the smooth running of any operation, and Leishman counted himself lucky in the personnel who surrounded him. Then, as now, the turnover of administrative staff at the Tattoo was extremely small. Indeed, one member of staff, Janet Begrie, had been with the Tattoo from the very beginning, at the age of 16, remaining over a period of forty years, on and off, to allow for the bringing up of a family. Her successor, Susan Lawton, who took over and continues in the role of Box Office Manager (sometimes more aptly called Ticket Services Manager) to this day has already clocked up eighteen years of sterling service. The reality of this had everything to do with job satisfaction and with the challenge of the event, every year being different.

From Bavaria in 1979 came The Brassband Munchen-Feldmoching with the dancing group of the Folklore Group 'Riadastoana'. The Parish of Feldmoching had been independent in former times, but in 1938 was incorporated into the City of Munich, which was twinned with Edinburgh.

Under its Musical Director Heinz Wohlmuth, President of the Musical Society of Upper and Lower Bavaria, the members of The Brassband Munchen-Feldmoching wore traditional costumes, the men in embroidered leather shorts, green waistless jackets, grey knitted cardigans and green Tyrolean hats featuring eagle fluff or a tuft of chamois hair. The girls wore plain, long woollen skirts, black waistbands with silver ornaments, aprons, and linen or silk neckerchiefs. The traditional 'Landler' and polka dances were performed including the 'Schuhplattler' dance, handed down from generation to generation in oral tradition. The folklore group 'Isargau', whose members came from various Bavarian and Munich groups, also performed polka dances and the historic 'Star-dance'.

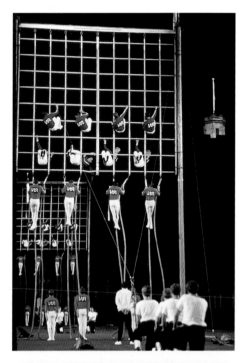

12.1 and 12.2 Two exciting displays at the 1979 Tattoo. (*left*) The Royal Navy Display Team and (*below*) The Royal Artillery Motor Cycle Display Team

Coinciding with all this colour and movement was a return visit after two years from The Pipes and Drums of The Royal Irish Rangers. Co-operating with Queen's University in Belfast, twelve young soldiers in saffron kilts and green tunics were accompanied by twelve girl students in traditional costumes to dance an Irish jig.

Then following this, twelve couples chosen from the Scottish Universities danced *Mairi's Wedding* to music provided by the Pipe Band of The Argyll and Sutherland Highlanders. In this case, the Scottish girls wore white dresses with the sashes of varying tartans

12.3 The Emperor Napoleon played in 1982 by 'Mountie' Joe Roberts

while their partners wore the tartans of the various universities: Hunting Stewart for Edinburgh and Tayforth, Gordon for Aberdeen, stronghold of The Gordon Highlanders, and Mackenzie for Strathclyde, home territory of The Royal Highland Fusiliers.

Making its first Tattoo appearance in 1980 was The Royal Band of HM The Sultan of Oman. Until the discovery of vast oilfields under the desert, the state of Oman had been virtually unknown in the Western world. A proud, deeply religious people, they had remained fiercely independent despite their new found wealth which had propelled them almost overnight into the twentieth century.

However, it was no coincidence that HM Sultan Qaboos Bin Said, who came to the throne of Oman in 1970, was educated in Britain, then qualified at The Royal Military Academy, Sandhurst, before serving as an officer with The Cameronians (Scottish Rifles). It goes without saying that this history was significant in his decision that the first performance of his personal Royal Band outside the Arabian Gulf States should take place in Scotland.

Thus over one hundred musicians, forming a pipe and military band, trained by the Director of Music, Lieutenant Colonel Tom

Crichton, formerly of The Argyll and Sutherland Highlanders, were to be found in the Edinburgh wind wearing Omani costume, the head cloth worn as a turban. With long green coats and red trousers, each man wore at his waist the khanjah, a curved knife which is the equivalent of the Highland dirk. The pipers wore the Douglas tartan plaid of the Cameronians, while an additional treat was the performance of a traditional Arab dance by a troop of boy and girl dancers, something rarely seen except by invited guests at Arab festivities.

Following this remarkable display was an equally impressive re-enactment on the castle battlements by soldiers of the 1st Battalion The Gordon Highlanders and riflemen of the 1st Battalion, 2nd KEO Gurkha Rifles of an initiative which had taken place at Dargai in India, in 1897. In that year, British control of the North West Frontier between India and Afghanistan was put to its severest test. Lieutenant Colonel David Murray gave the following account in the programme notes of 1980:

The establishment of an agreed national frontier had spread fears amongst the fierce and warlike Pathan clansmen of the Border that the British intended to occupy all the tribal territories up to the frontier and so deprive them of their ancestral lands and their traditional independence.

Fierce fighting broke out in the North, and quickly spread. The Khyber Pass was lost, but operations on a large scale by the British and Indian Armies gradually restored order. After four months, the British were ready to deal with the last area of resistance south of the Khyber Pass, where lived the brave and well-armed Afridis in the broad and fertile valleys of Tirah, where no conqueror had ever set foot.

The Afridis greatly outnumbered the British and, for the first time, were almost as well armed with modern rifles. The opening phase of the operation called for the British to dislodge the tribesmen from the village of Dargai which, standing on beetling cliffs scaled only by a single precipitous footpath, dominated the track leading to the Tirah. On the morning of 29 October, the British, led by the 1st Battalion,

12.4 A display of bridge building Engineers

12.5 (*overleaf*) Men of the 1st Batallion The Royal Scots (The Royal Regiment) celebrate the Regiment's 350th Anniversary in 1983 by dancing with the ladies of the Royal Scottish Country Dance society

2nd Gurkhas, advanced towards the heights, already a position of great natural strength and now strengthened further by stone breast-works held by more than twelve thousand Afridis, banners flying, drums beating and surnais (the local bagpipe) playing as they shouted their defiance.

The moment the Gurkhas left cover they were halted by rapid fire. The British artillery was ineffective among the rocks, and for five hours the Gurkhas tried to reach the foot of the cliffs. Finally, The Gordon Highlanders were ordered up. When the moment to advance came, their Colonel had addressed them: 'The General says the hill must be taken at all costs – The Gordon Highlanders will take it!'

What followed was to be described as 'the most spectacular attack in the whole of British Frontier history'. Pipes playing, the Gordons stormed forward. The Gurkhas joined them as they passed, and together they charged the bullet swept ground and swarmed up the

sides of the steep hill. 'Stiff climb!' panted the Colonel. 'Ye're gaun verra strong for an auld man!' replied a Gordon, slapping his Commanding Officer on the back in admiration.

The tussle for the heights was soon over, but during the advance the Gordons lost one officer and six men, and six officers and thirty five men were wounded. Piper Findlater, although shot through both ankles, propped himself up on a rock and continued to play, *The Cock of the North*, for which he was later awarded the Victoria Cross.

Although peace never reigned for long on the frontier afterwards, a mutual respect did emerge between the British and the Patans, enduring until the British left India, both sides perhaps remembering the Eastern saying, 'The courage of your enemies does you honour.'

Lieutenant-General Sir David Young, who was now GOC Scotland, had known Leslie Dow since 1945 at the Officer Cadet Training Unit, then as a fellow student at Staff College. The 1980 Tattoo included The Big Brown Music Machine, a very large marching band from the University of California with both male and female members, drum majorettes and a very large sound. The complete band was accommodated in one of the barrack blocks at Craigiehall, to the north of Edinburgh, and Dow confided in him that there were concerns because these were young students, not military personnel, and it might be difficult to keep them under control.

Happily, such fears were unfounded. 'They were a great bunch,' recalled Sir David. 'The chief drum majorette never dropped her baton once although it seemed to disappear through the clouds from time to time, and the only problem at Craigiehall was caused by the music from rehearsals which diverted the attention of the staff from their work!'

But you must also remember that this was Presbyterian Edinburgh and Sir David did receive a letter from a lady member of the audience who complained that the female performers were showing far too much bare leg.

12.6 The Junior Leaders
Regiment Royal Artillery
give a display at the 1984
Tattoo

The chief drum majorette of The Big Brown Machine may not have dropped her baton once, but Pipe Major Stuart D. Samson of The 1st Battalion Gordon Highlanders, who was making his Tattoo debut as a 14-year-old, remembered another less fortunate incident.

He had only ever seen the event on the television before and was amazed at how small the Esplanade was, and how little room there was between the ranks when the massed pipes and drums marched up and down. There was one evening in particular he would never forget, when a final counter march took place at the bottom of the Esplanade before the Pipes and Drums headed back up the slope and into the Castle.

As the pipes were moving through between the drummers, one of the tenor drummers got his drumstick caught up in the ribbons of a

12.7 The Royal Band of HM The Sultan of Oman

piper's drones so that his arm was suddenly pulled in the opposite direction. Rather than try to get rid of his stick, which would have been difficult since it was connected to his hand by a cord wrapped around his fingers to enable him to twirl it, he gave an almighty tug which pulled the entire set of bagpipes from the shoulders of the astonished piper.

# 13  Goat's Cheese and Penguins

NORWEGIAN guardsmen are famous for having enormous appetites, but they are choosy. After a second week in exile they invariably asked for more milk, more brown bread, a fourth meal a day, if possible. After the first visit of The Kongen's Garde in 1961, it became a tradition for large quantities of Norwegian goat's milk cheese to be brought with them to keep them going. In 1982, they even went so far as to try and encourage some of the other regiments to try some, but without success.

It was obvious the Italians, English and Scots, even the Gurkhas, were unimpressed, so the Norwegians put it about that each of them was in the habit of eating at least 250 grams of this goat's milk cheese before every performance, and that this was the secret of their extra-ordinary reserves of energy.

When the story went the rounds, Nils Egelien and his guardsmen thought this hilarious. 'One evening we placed five or six small groups outside Redford Barracks accommodation where the Tattoo buses were stacked up. The groups sat there at the side of the road slicing up and eating goat's milk cheese in full view of everybody just so that they could see that everything the Norwegians had told them was true!' he laughed.

The Norwegians' reputation for eccentricity took a further step when that same year they officially upgraded the penguin at Edinburgh Zoo they had made a lance corporal in 1972 to the rank of sergeant. 'Our visits to Edinburgh were always wonderfully memorable,' said Nils Egelien.

The Kongen's Garde were back in 1989, the year Egelien was to retire, and after four Tattoos it was said that he had become more

13.1 and 13.2 (*above*) The Edinburgh Military Tattoo tartan, the original design and (*above right*) the fiftieth anniversary tartan (see page 184)

Scots than Norwegian. Because of this, E.H. Marchant, commandant of the Edinburgh Training Centre, was conscripted to kit him out in full Highland dress in the official Edinburgh Military Tattoo tartan, which had been introduced in 1983. This was achieved by gaining access to Egelien's room at the barracks and taking measurements from his uniform when he was elsewhere. On the day of the presentation, the outfit was paraded and handed over on a tailor's dummy. Egelien was delighted.

Since then, the official Edinburgh Military Tattoo tartan and Edinburgh Military Tattoo dress tartan have become almost fashion accessories for both participants and audiences at the Tattoo, worn as kilts, trews, waistcoats and scarves. Registered with the Design Registry of the Patent Office and recorded with The Scottish Tartans Society and the Museum of Scottish Tartans, both tartans incorporate the colours of the three services, the Navy (navy blue), the Army (red), the Royal Air Force (sky blue) and the City of Edinburgh (black and white). In 1999, an updated tartan design was introduced to celebrate the Tattoo's fiftieth anniversary.

Behind the scenes there was always a sense of fun involving both the visitors and those who welcomed them. In 1985, the captain of The Queen's Guard Rutgers was accompanied by his wife, and E.H. Marchant heard through the grapevine that the couple had been longing to have children, but so far without success.

'During the course of my rounds I heard they were not too happy with the twin beds in their room,' he said. 'So thanks to Barrack Services, quite unbeknown to them, a large double bed was obtained and installed during the rehearsal period. Shortly after their return to the United States, we received a letter from Bob. Sandi was pregnant, and he made the promise that if it was a boy, it would be called Redford!' said Marchant. 'It was a girl. We slipped up. The bed had been facing south!'

In 1986, Marchant recalled going to meet the Herresmusikkorps 300 at Turnhouse Airport, and found the aircraft waiting, but the band prevented from disembarking until the beer and wine which had been stored aft was unloaded.

The reason for this, he explained, was to maintain the balance. Had the passengers been allowed to disembark before the stores were

13.3  A Fox armoured car of The Royal Scots Dragoon Guards

unloaded, the Luftwaffe were convinced that the rear of the aircraft with its huge weight of alcohol would have tilted the front of the aircraft off the ground.

That year, he recalled, they had an age span of seventy-one years quartered at the Edinburgh Training Centre, the youngest performer being four years old, the oldest, seventy-five. Both celebrated their birthdays during the run.

Major Christine Barton's first year as Foreign Contingent Liaison Officer was in 1988, and it fell to her to calm down the semi-hysterical artistic director of the Ensemble of the Hungarian People's Army on their arrival at Edinburgh Airport to find that the dancers were required to carry their own suitcases.

During the Festival Cavalcade it was decided that the five Desert Rats, with the average age of seventy, who had accompanied the Tobruk contingent, should be allowed to take part in the Festival Cavalcade, but it was agreed that the entire route would be too long for them to manage on foot. It was therefore decided at the last moment that Major Barton would lead them past the saluting dais, then 'peel off' behind the Royal Scottish Academy building at the front of which the platform was situated.

This was achieved with precision, but as they started to move away, a horse box which had somehow become part of the procession slowed down to offer them a lift. 'It was a sheer delight,' she recalled. 'The Rats were able to wave and talk to the crowds, and one of them shouted out, "They might think we're old nags, but there's life in us yet!"'

Barton's problems with the Hungarians were not over, and she was later obliged to explain to the male dancers based at the barracks that it was inappropriate in mixed sex accommodation to walk naked from their rooms to the shower facilities and display what a member of the Australian contingent was describing as 'their dried flower arrangements'.

And towards the end of the run she remembered watching the incredulous faces of the Hungarian female dancers as they arrived at

13.4 (*overleaf*) The Band of The Royal Marines, 1983

the officers' mess of The Gordon Highlanders for a toga party. 'The sight of British army officers in white bed sheets, sporrans, regimental bow ties, Blues Brothers hats and sunglasses, and Doc Marten boots completely baffled them,' she said. 'It was hilarious.'

But the Hungarians soon entered into the spirit of it all. Commentator Tom Fleming often repeated the story of the Guard Commander of The Gordon Highlanders who was told by one of the dancers, 'You are very pretty'.

'No, my dear,' replied the Guard Commander. 'You are pretty. I am smart!'

# 14   Lasting Friendships

THE South Australia Police Band has the proud tradition of being the first police band formed in Australia. Since 1884, it had become an integral part of the South Australia Police Department and was held in high esteem by the local community, so much so that Alistair McHaigh, a well-known Scots expatriate in Adelaide, decided to bring it to the attention of Colonel Dow, who went to see the band perform for himself on a visit to Adelaide in 1987.

When Dow gave the go-ahead for them to come to Edinburgh, the Police Department, determined to provide a dazzling spectacle, then invited the world champion Australian Drill Team, a group of young ladies aged between fifteen and twenty-two years, to join them. The police band totalled forty-six in number, whilst the Australian Drill team had forty-seven, thus making a combined total of ninety-three.

Meanwhile, the South Australian Government whilst totally supportive, advised that they were unable to offer financial assistance other than to meet the salaries of the band members. However, such was the group's determination to go, that within two years, through setting up a major lottery in which two cars were offered as prizes, then special performances and support from local industry, media and the community, they had raised the necessary funds.

'The desire was for the performance to be all Australian in its music and parade activities,' said Superintendent John White, the band's commanding officer. 'So Drum Major Sergeant Ken Ekin of the police band, and Mrs Lyn Edwards-Ferrauto of the drill team, set about creating the drill movements, whilst Senior Constable Roger Downtown, the band's music arranger, under the leadership of Ernie Alderslade, musical director, set about arranging a totally Australian spectacular. Unfortunately, before they set off Ernie Alderslade had to step down owing to ill health, and Retired Wing Commander Eric Banks, a previous Tattoo director of music who had recently moved to live in Adelaide, stepped into the breach.'

In the meantime, the drill team 'mums' had been busy making costumes and a large Australian flag. Lyn Edwards-Ferrauto and Sergeant Ekin had also come up with the idea of a large kangaroo pounding onto the Esplanade, so they created 'Adelaide' the kangaroo with the oversized pouch. A local store built and donated the outfit, and Senior Sergeant Ken Gunn, the tour administrator, was persuaded to wear it. Over the course of the Tattoo he lost several pounds in weight through perspiration.

'It was an unqualified success,' said Superintendent White. 'The band left Adelaide in July 1990 as an unknown group outside of Australia, and returned home in September 1990 with its reputation and tradition finally stamped internationally. The only sadness on our return was the sudden death of Assistant Commissioner Kevin Harvey, APM, who had accompanied us and whose leadership and dedication had been a major contribution towards making the trip possible.'

Queen Victoria School in Dunblane is Scotland's National Memorial to those who gave their lives in the South African Wars of the latter half of the nineteenth century. By an accident of history, it is funded by the Ministry of Defence, and all of its pupils must be Scots and sons of the services.

Today it is a mixed sex boarding school, but during the 1980s it was all male, guarding jealously its parade uniforms and ceremonial traditions. Its curriculum differed little from other Scottish schools except that the boys, who joined at the age of ten plus, were required to spend three hours a week for their first two terms learning the basics of foot drill to enable them to take part in the school's ceremonial occasions; in addition, for their two years in the primary department, they were, and continue to be, encouraged to learn the pipes, drums or Highland dancing as part of their timetable.

When they move into the senior school at the age of twelve plus, these activities become entirely voluntary, but the seeds have been sown and as much as fifty per cent may continue through most of their school career. Both pipe band and dancers have an international reputation; the former particularly because of their regular appearances at the Scottish Rugby Union's stadium at Murrayfield before and during international matches.

An invitation to perform at the Tattoo was first made in the early summer of 1985 and caused great excitement. But it was not that simple, explained Brigadier O.R. Tweedy, 'On age alone, less than one third of the boys at the school would still be available for 1990, and many others who could well be involved might not yet have arrived.'

As a result, over one hundred proformas were sent out to parents of those who would still be at the school. All were returned and only one refused to give unqualified support. 'We therefore had a clear mandate to start to plan for an event to take place four and a half years later,' said Brigadier Tweedy.

Fortunately, the boys thought the prospect of taking part in something as prestigious as the Tattoo was a worthwhile challenge, and fears of not achieving enough volunteers of the right standard were unfounded. As one ten-year old put it when asked why he had volunteered to learn to dance in late 1988, 'I wanted to take part, but I knew that I couldn't learn enough to do it as a piper or drummer, but if I worked hard I should get there as a dancer.' Get there he did.

Having established that the target of a band of forty-five and twenty-five dancers could be achieved, the next challenge was to ensure that enthusiasm and standards were maintained throughout the four week period. The beginning was considered relatively easy, but to keep the momentum going over two dress rehearsals and twenty-four performances was another matter. Fortunately, according to Brigadier Tweedy, the two golden principles of running a boarding school came to their aid: 'Feed them well and keep them busy'.

Although feeding them at Redford Barracks would not have been a problem, separate accommodation and a canteen would have needed to be provided. The more the subject was discussed, the more it became apparent that the right answer would be for the boys to be based at the school in Dunblane and commute. This would involve two hours travelling every day, but this inconvenience was far outweighed by the benefits of the school providing the cooks and accommodation, a swimming pool, and almost unlimited sports facilities, not to mention the familiar environment and an adult staff with whom they were all familiar.

By early 1990, all plans were agreed, and halfway through the Easter term parents were circulated with ninety names from whom the final team of seventy was chosen, allowing anyone to withdraw who might want to. Only one did, but there was also one learner piper who was mortally offended at not being included on the list.

When he demanded to know why, Pipe Major Allan Dippie told him in the nicest possible way that he simply was not good enough, whereupon he stormed from the office on the verge of tears to re-appear at the start of the Summer term having perfected the entire programme including *Memories*, the popular Andrew Lloyd Webber song from the musical *Cats*, which some of the older pipers had not even started upon.

And so it was that on the afternoon of 27 July 1990, seventy young men, something over one third of the Senior School, assembled in Dunblane. The youngest was eleven-and-a-half and the oldest two weeks short of his eighteenth birthday. That evening was devoted to last minute checks on uniform, replacing outgrown items and those that had been lost, sorting out the pipes, most of which had not been played for the four weeks of the holiday, and setting up the brand new side drums.

According to Brigadier Tweedy, some pretty encouraging discoveries were made on arrival at Edinburgh Castle. 'Young Victorians were

14.1  Maori dancers appearing in 1975

not the only ones who were not note perfect, and the Australian Ladies World Champion Drill Team contained some absolute smashers!'

Over the next few days rehearsals were long and hard, and it soon became clear that the Victorians' immediate predecessors in the show, the United States Marine Corps Band from Quantico, were setting an incredibly high standard, while the girls from Adelaide were quite breathtaking. The Victorians even began wondering if they were good enough, but their answer came with a spontaneous rumble of applause from the other performers at the first full rehearsal.

After that it was all routine. 'One hour on the bus and a walk up the hill to the Army School of Piping to await the time to tune up and form up ready for our cue,' said Tweedy. 'Eight minutes, twenty-five seconds of limelight, and off under the East Stand to be joined shortly afterwards by the girls from Adelaide. Then there were barely fifteen minutes for the band, but rather longer for the dancers, before it was necessary to disentangle themselves, adjust dress, remove signs of lipstick and assemble for the finale.'

There were lasting friendships with the City of Adelaide. For some of the boys the final performance was delivered covered in lipstick and wearing somebody else's head dress; for others, there were memories of the Boy Pipe Major's eighteenth birthday party, and the almost hysterical 15-year-old piper arrested by the military police on the last night for having a condom on his base drone. To this day the originator of this prank probably has no idea how long it took the Pipe Major to calm down the recipient and persuade him to see the funny side of it.

Whatever their lasting memories, on the morning of Sunday 2 September, seventy tired but elated young men dispersed having spent fifty-eight hours on their buses travelling the equivalent distance of Dunblane to the heel of Italy. Nine of them were saying goodbye to school life and going off to their universities or chosen careers, and the balance returned to their families for two days recuperation before returning to school again for the autumn term. It had been a triumph.

The director of music of the Republic of Singapore Police Force, Idris b Mohd Yusof, had decided, somewhat bravely, not only to combine his military band with his three Pipes and Drums contingents and have them play together, but also to incorporate popular Chinese, Malay and Indian music into a unique blend along with one or two well-known and well-loved Scottish tunes heard each year at the Tattoo. Bruce Mackenzie Niven, Deputy Assistant Commissioner of Police of the Gurkha Contingent of the Singapore Police Force said, 'To all these "Sounds of Singapore", as we were to christen our item in 1991, we were able to add, by way of a complete contrast, the stark cacophony of the cymbals and drums that accompany any Chinese Lion Dance Troup.'

14.2 (*opposite*) Maori dancer from Kapaka, New Zealand, 2000

'The uniforms of the members of our male and female band contingents were both handsome and attractive and were extremely colourful under the arc lights, with the red tartans of the lady pipers in pleasing contrast to their green velvet doublets, and with the white tunics of the male bandsmen standing out vividly beside the midnight blue of the plaids of the Gurkha pipers, the heavy gold and silver thread of the colourful pipe banners and the glitter and sparkle from the drummers' belts and the highly polished leather of the casbards of the Gurkhas' "kukris".'

Nevertheless, Foreign Contingent Liaison Officer Major Christine Barton was despatched to purchase fifty sets of thermal underwear, extra small, for the Singapore lady pipers and dancers.

To this spectacle were to be added the colourful ethnic costumes of the people of Singapore singing to the assembled audience as the massed Singapore bands, still in total darkness, slow marched into the arena from the Castle drawbridge. Then with a crescendo of noise, the massed bands broke into quick time, the search lights flooded the arena, and the Singapore contingent marched down the Esplanade as a strong, stirring spectacle of colour and movement.

However, according to Bruce Mackenzie Niven, one or two major problems had to be addressed during the work-up period. First there was a division of opinion amongst the musicians as to the effect (or lack of effect) of having coloured lights attached to the headdress of each performer, which could be switched on and off and functioned using batteries carried in breast pockets and sporrans.

Seen on the parade square at the Police Academy in Singapore, these coloured lights created a superb effect in complete darkness, but others felt that without the arc lights on them, the colour and spectacle would be lost. In the end, somebody said, 'What's the point of travelling 10,000 miles to Edinburgh just to turn the lights out!' So the lights went on and, of course, the BBC in particular were delighted with the consequent brilliance of the scene.

Then a second problem arose over the format of the four to five minute item scheduled to follow the band display. Originally it had been intended to use a troupe of Chinese performers whose act involved them balancing thirty-foot high flag poles in the palms of their hands, then on their knees, chests, shoulders, chins and foreheads before tossing the upright pole to a fellow performer to repeat the performance.

Now of course in Singapore winds generally only blow immediately before a tropical rainstorm, and for most of the time there is no wind. The Gurkhas were thus faced with two difficulties. How could they prevent these large flags with poles and acrobats attached from flying off the castle ramparts during a Scottish 'blow', and how would they be able to fit thirty feet long wooden poles into the luggage compartment of an Airbus 300 or 747 to bring them to the UK?

So poles were written out and a lion dance was written in. Even then, there was concern that the heads of the lions would get sodden if there was a downpour. Such lion heads are intricately designed. Ears flap and eyes and mouths open and close during a performance when manipulated by the artistes inside.

14.3 Dancers from the Central Band of the Russian Navy

If the mouth did not open then the artiste could not see where he was going, and thus there was an outside chance that he and his partner in the tail of the lion might have somehow fallen off the Esplanade and ended up in Princes Street Gardens below. In addition, as the finale of the Singapore item, one of the lions was scripted to make a bit of a play when meeting up with the fire-breathing guardian dragon from the castle, emerging from its lair in the form of a Lothian Fire Brigade fire-engine heavily disguised as a very large, green metallic dragon.

Again, the driver of this monster could neither see very well out of the mouth of his dragon as it spouted fire and flames, nor was there much room for manoeuvre, so there was a distinct possibility of the lion's head becoming severely singed, if not actually ending up inside the fire-engine.

The Gurkhas required thirty-five very sharp and very large Gurkha 'kukris', and two M16 rifles for the Castle sentries to carry during the Singapore display. This meant not only applying for 'overflying rights' for lethal weapons from the various countries that lay under the flight path from Singapore to Edinburgh, but also that the rifles were required to be de-activated while in transit in strict accordance with the stringent conditions laid down by the British Home Office.

14.4 Dancers of the Fiji Military Forces Band

Once in Edinburgh, two Gurkha sentries were deployed to stand guard over Edinburgh Castle, and having retrieved their M16 rifles from the Home Office, set out to rehearse. The rifles worked splendidly, but unfortunately the Gurkhas, small in stature, soon discovered that their heavily studded boots just could not cope with the slippery and inclined cobblestones of the castle's drawbridge and surrounding area.

When obliged to halt, gravity and the array of well-burnished studs on the soles of their boots decreed that they continued to move forward some three to four yards before coming to a halt. Elastoplast and various types of masking tape were tried out over the offending studs, but eventually the boots had to be sent to a cobbler and the studs removed. Most humiliating.

Nothing is ever as easy as it looks and often seems. With participants arriving from different countries and with language barriers, misunderstandings inevitably arose. Thankfully, though, they were always resolved. On the afternoon of a dress rehearsal, with the first public performance scheduled to take place the following day, Colonel Dow asked Brigadier Iain Reid, commander of 52 Lowland Brigade, to go with him to try and fend off a walk out by an international contingent which had become worked up over some diplomatic incident. With portable telephone lines humming between Edinburgh, the Foreign Office and various ambassadors abroad, the meeting took place along the following lines:

'We want to go home NOW.'

'No, we want you to be on the buses at 6pm for the rehearsal.'

'We are going home NOW.'

'No, we think we should all let our governments discuss this and in the meantime we want you on the buses at 6pm.'

'No, we are expecting instructions from home by phone.'

'We very much want you on the buses by 6pm, even if the telephone does not ring.'

'OK.'

Needless to say, they were on the buses at 6pm, stayed for the

14.5 (*opposite*) Aboriginal dancer, 2000

entire run, and wrote afterwards to say that they had enjoyed themselves enormously. That's show business.

When Brigadier Iain Reid asked Arena Master Jim Macfarlane what it took to do his job, he was told, 'The ability to influence members of the cast at a range of about fifty yards without moving your lips, Sir!'

And always there was laughter. One of Brigadier Reid's guests, an elderly and rather grand lady, was introduced to Castle adjutant Robin Cole who was wearing full uniform and police radio earphones. 'How sad for such a young officer to need a hearing aid,' she said. All was later explained.

By way of an introduction to the 1991 TV coverage, Ian Christie, the director, decided to lead off with an interview with Lieutenant Colonel Leslie Dow on his final Tattoo as producer. He knew Dow would be secretly thrilled to meet Kate Adie, the BBC's chief news correspondent, so arranged for her to ask the questions. Given her formidable reputation for reporting from the world's trouble spots, Kate was the one media person whom the officers and men of the British Armed Forces could immediately relate to with both affection and respect. It nevertheless caused quite a stir in the Castle gatehouse that evening when she used it as her make-up room.

# 15 ~~~ Scenes

BERT Donaldson was in charge of Edinburgh District Council's Special Duties Section and was technical consultant to the Tattoo from 1956 until his death in 1986. Cath, his wife, had first been to the Tattoo in 1955 with her mother, and when she got home, she gave him all the details. 'I won't be going to that. I've had enough square bashing to do me for the rest of my life!' he said.

How wrong he was. The following year he joined Edinburgh Corporation's City Architect's Department as an electrical inspector, and almost immediately his duties involved inspecting the Tattoo's electrics, which from then on grew and grew.

Supervising the erection of the new stands in 1976, Bert found the bits would not go together, though they had done so perfectly the previous year on arrival from the manufacturers. The whole timetable of the show was threatened as the stands absolutely refused to go up.

He finally discovered that when the stands had been put into storage the previous year, someone had not followed the computer-generated system. The complex structure was designed to cope with the fourteen foot drop from the top of the Esplanade to the bottom and the parts were not interchangeable. It took Bert and his team a considerable time to sort out the puzzle, but sort it they did, as was his way. Thereafter, his Tattoo responsibilities escalated. He could arrange the appropriate stabling for camels and elephants as capably as he ensured that the Tattoo's various flashes, bangs and crashes remained well within fire regulations.

15.1 Bert Donaldson

It was said of Bert Donaldson that he could create, acquire, or improvise anything. For one Tattoo he got hold of two RAF fighter aircraft to sit on the Castle ramparts. Unfortunately, at the end of the run, one Spitfire unaccountably went missing and since Bert had personally signed for it, the RAF sent him a bill for several hundred thousands of pounds.

Poor Bert. No matter how hard he insisted that the aeroplane had been returned in good order, the authorities flatly refused to believe him. It was a harrowing experience for the Tattoo's 'Mr Fix-It', but fortunately, the Spitfire finally turned up behind a shed on an RAF base in England just before sheriff officers were scheduled to recover the 'debt' from him.

On Bert's death in 1986, the role of technical consultant was taken on by his assistant, the equally enterprising Ian MacFadyen. Ian had learned his craft well and the adage 'the show must go on' to this day remains a facet of his undoubted skill to get things done.

Iris Ritchie was married to a serving officer in the Royal Scots. When she and her husband moved from Glencorse Barracks to semi-detached quarters at Redford Barracks in 1952, they were fortunate in being able to employ an excellent household help, Mrs Milligan, whose husband Corporal Milligan was a very experienced piper, a regular at the Tattoo.

'The heavens opened that year, and one day I asked her about the uniforms,' said Iris Ritchie.

'Soaked through,' she replied.

From then on Iris and Mrs Milligan set up a drying room for uniforms. 'We finally decided to fix up a line over the boiler in the scullery which, apart from sometimes being hit in the face by a sleeve, was no problem,' said Iris.

Regimental Sergeant Majors are a breed apart, and it was said of Major Campbell Graham that he needed no telephone when talking to London from Edinburgh Castle. However, like many such individuals, he is best remembered for his heart of gold. Following his retirement in 1982 after thirty three years of service, he took over the running of Lady Haig's Poppy Factory in Edinburgh.

Although he had worked with the Tattoo for some years before, from 1980 Major Graham became the Tattoo's first official Arena Master and for three years thereafter was responsible for marshalling the cast on the Esplanade. 'I was brought in by Brigadier Sir Gregor Macgregor who wasn't satisfied that things were being done correctly,' he said. 'The Brigadier asked me what I needed to smarten things up? A couple of sergeants, I told him!'

However, perhaps his greatest moment of glory came in 1980 when somebody came up with the idea of lowering the lone piper from a helicopter onto the Castle battlements to play the last lament.

'It was proposed that Pipe Major MacDonald should report to the helicopter pad in Leuchars in Fife in full piping gear and be helicoptered to Edinburgh Castle during the children's performance on a Saturday when he would be lowered onto the battlements,' explained Campbell.

Lieutenant Colonel Murray, deputy producer, was aghast. What would happen if the helicopter crashed? 'We would lose one of our best pipers,' he exclaimed.

The Army School of Piping was also outraged that a valuable piper should be treated in such a cavalier fashion, and so it was decided that instead Major Graham, kitted out in full regimental dress, should stand in for him. Wearing underpants beneath his kilt which bore the slogan 'Join the Scots Guards!', he was winched down.

A swift substitution behind the ramparts of the Half Moon Battery then enabled the real piper, in identical uniform save for the underpants, to mount the platform and play with great aplomb. Nobody in the audience was any the wiser, although Campbell Graham still complains at the notion that he was expendable when the piper was not. But whether he had intended to or not, he had created a precedent. On another occasion, during the children's matinee, he was volunteered to be lowered over the Castle battlements and left hanging by his toes and fingernails. A mountain rescue helicopter was then summoned to lift him off.

15.2 When it was decided that the lone piper should be lowered onto the Castle battlements Campbell Graham had to take the place of the actual piper – the Army School of Piping could not risk losing one of its best pipers!

'I was never more pleased to have a strong pair of hairy legs wrapped around my waist as I was winched up into the helicopter,' he said. 'Then after waving to all the children I was dropped on the Meadows on the south side of the city to the astonishment of passers by, and had to make my way back to the castle on foot! You have to be tough when you work for the Tattoo.'

15.3 Pipe Major Angus Mac-
Donald (*left*) and his substitute
Major Campbell Graham (*right*)

Graham was, and continues to be, a strict disciplinarian. 'When I
was appointed Arena Marshall I changed two things,' he announced.
'The first was that the three nearby pubs, The Ensign Ewart, Deacon
Brodies and The Castle Arms, were out of bounds during performances. Secondly, I stopped the mass exodus by the audience prior
to the playing of the National Anthems. All stewards were instructed
to prevent anybody leaving their seat before the finale.'

On one occasion, he was standing at attention for the salute during
the British National Anthem when he noticed a steward being pushed
to the side by a man making his way down the aisle with a small boy.
He immediately accosted the individual to be informed that the small
boy needed to visit the toilet. 'In future you should organise your
son's toileting to avoid the anthems,' barked the Major in response.

During the Falklands War in 1982, the Tattoo found itself short of
pipers and enlisted help from the university pipe bands. On this occasion Graham was doing the rounds and appalled at the appearance of
one of the pipers snapped, 'Get your hair cut. You look like a lassie!'

'But Sir, I am a lassie,' the piper retorted.

'Well, get tidied up anyway,' continued the Major beating a rapid retreat.

Characters abounded. Colonel Douglas Spratt came to Edinburgh in an anti-aircraft unit during World War Two and was to become the longest serving member of the Tattoo's production team. However, although he joined at the very start, it was not until 1967 that he was credited as being 'in charge of searchlights'.

Of course in a strictly military sense, they were not searchlights, rather 'follow spotlights'. In any event, 'follow spotlights' were soon to accumulate, particularly between 1968 until 1990 while he held the post of lighting director, and afterwards when his former assistant Captain Ian Scott took over with Spratt remaining a consultant until 1991.

Douglas Spratt was adamant that his volunteer lighting operators had the most hazardous job in the Tattoo, with little public recognition, but plenty of attention from the elements as they perched on their lofty lighting towers. What was even more remarkable was that he not only combined his Tattoo duties with being second in command of 432 (City of Edinburgh) Engineer Regiment, but in civilian life managed an Edinburgh bakery firm.

Lieutenant Colonel Ian McBain, who was a commentator between 1984 and 1991, always marvelled at how smoothly things ran in the production box. 'There was not much room for ad libbing as it was geared to slick production and quick changes of acts and performers. The commentary also provided the cues and we were all very aware that any changes could result in chaos in the arena.'

Colonel McBain's biggest *faux pas* was undoubtedly to thank the Bank of England for their sponsorship when it should have been the Bank of Scotland! He remained totally unaware of the error until after the performance when he was confronted by the looming figure of Major Brian Leishman.

However, the pre-show announcements gave some opportunity for originality and Colonel McBain always tried to raise a laugh from the audience with the nightly weather forecast. When Julia Barry left after seven years as the producer's secretary, a suitable announcement was made about her impending nuptials. 'As the pre-show band was playing *I'm Getting Married in the Morning* and other suitable music, Julia was found scrambling in the waste paper basket for the notes I had used in the announcement to put in her scrapbook!'

15.4 Leslie Dow (*left*) and Brian Leishman (*right*) with secretary Julia Barry

At one rehearsal McBain recalled Leslie Dow commenting upon some rather lovely high-kicking dancers who were accompanying an American University Band and finished his comments with, '. . . and ladies and gentlemen, we will be seeing a lot more of those girls later.'

Of course, as referred to in Chapter 4, with Ian McBain, it was a family affair.

In 1967, Ian was appointed Deputy Assistant Adjutant General of HQ Scottish Command, and his responsibilities included ceremonial in Scotland including the administration of the Tattoo. Eight years later his brother Stuart, by then a major, assumed the same appointment at HQ Scotland with similar responsibilities and four years later took over as Assistant Adjutant General in HQ The Scottish Division with responsibility for arranging the availability of the Pipes and Drums and military bands of the Scottish Regiments at the Tattoo.

In 1983, Lieutenant-Colonels Stuart and Ian McBain retired from the Army and both took up retired officer appointments in Edinburgh Castle. This coincided with there being a requirement for an assistant commentator for the Tattoo, and Leslie Dow persuaded them both to volunteer.

15.5 Spot the difference: Lieutenant-Colonels Stuart and Ian McBain

This was the first time that this duty had been shared by two people, but it made little difference. Being identical twins, their voices were so similar it was virtually impossible to tell them apart. Indeed, bets were often placed as to which one it was performing on a particular night. Even the BBC gave up insisting that it should be the same twin commentating over the three nights when they were filming. The Dow/McBain triumvirate in the Tattoo's control box was to last for eight years when all three retired together.

Marshalling was the Territorial Army's contribution to the Tattoo, recruiting from the infantry TA units in Edinburgh, which included the Edinburgh University Officer Training Corps.

Colonel G. 'Timber' Wood of The Argyll and Sutherland Highlanders first became involved when he became Camp Commandant at HQ Scotland in 1974. 'Being Chief Marshall was part of the job specification,' he said. 'When I moved to Stirling Castle as Regimental Secretary of The Argyll and Sutherland

Highlanders, Leslie Dow and David Murray invoked the Old Pals Act, and I carried on. However, as I was now a volunteer I could not claim the HQ Scotland perk of a long lie-in in the morning, which combined with commuting the forty odd miles to Edinburgh at the end of a full day at RHQ meant very long hours.'

He still found the experience very enjoyable. 'The biggest problem was collecting the numbers required, one for each entrance at every performance. As I tried to contact those who had taken part the year before, I would discover that some of them had left the TA, or were too busy, or had left Edinburgh. The problem was then to find new blood to replace them, which I did through asking Adjutants and Training Officers. Amazingly, once a roster was published, I was never let down by an absentee.'

There were, however, some dramatic moments. One night Liz Henderson, an officer with Tayforth OTC, who commuted nightly from Arbroath to help with the marshalling, was covering the coal yard entrance when she was struck by a plastic ball the size of a grapefruit during the firework display. It was part of an enormous sky burst, and she was rushed off by medics, fortunately with no lasting damage.

On another occasion, a motorbike from the Royal Air Force team skidded and roared onto its side into a crash barrier behind which a number of wheel chair spectators had been positioned so as to have a better view. They certainly got one, but fortunately nobody was injured.

From the early days, the provision of accommodation for the many regiments and band visitors became an increasingly more important consideration. By 1981, it had become a major challenge. E.H. Marchant took over as Commandant of the Edinburgh Training Centre that year, and one of his first visitors was Lieutenant-Colonel Dow. 'We had met at Sandhurst in 1963,' recalled Marchant, 'in fact, we played hockey together. He at left back and I at left half.'

Leslie explained the problem. How to accommodate the cast of the Tattoo under one roof? Marchant had previously attended the Tattoo

with the Sandhurst contingent in 1964 and had been based at the Sailors' Hostel which stood where the city's St James Centre now stands. He readily agreed to take over responsibility for housing the entire cast, including the women.

'From the outset it required total commitment, not only on my part, but by the whole of my staff including our casual workers,' he said. 'We were aware that since the cast would be spending at least eighteen hours of every day in the barracks, boredom easily builds up unless we did everything we could to combat it.'

There were other problems of a more ethnic variety to be confronted, for example, the designing and fitting of Asian-style sanitary ware which is different from the European variety. Fortunately, with financial assistance from Oman, this was achieved, and the appropriate loos continue to be held in store to be fitted whenever Muslims arrive to take part in the Tattoo. That same year Marchant was also called upon to provide a Mosque at Redford, which he was able to do by calling upon the local Mutawa to bless a building which went on to cater for 1320 Omanis.

15.7 The stewards are an essential part of the Tattoo

Every Tattoo performer is served four meals a day, and on double performance nights an inter-performance snack is available. All of the food until recently was prepared at Redford Barracks. 'The catering empire never slept,' said Marchant. Quantities of various items were needed, for example 16, 750 eggs, 2,327 yards of sausages which if laid starting from the Esplanade would reach Holyrood Palace and back to the City Chambers, 11,250 loaves of bread, and 11,250 pounds of meat and fish. Since changing to a civilian contract, these stores are purchased locally, adding to the revenue generated by the Festival and the Tattoo for the city.

15.8 (*opposite*) The Finale as seen from a balloon

# 16 Scaffolding and Noises Off

TUBULAR scaffolding was used for the construction of the Tattoo's spectator stands for a period of twenty-five years. It was the understanding of James Sibbald, Tattoo Joint-Secretary and Company Secretary until 1990, that the supplier arranged for its annual requirements of new tubular scaffolding for the whole of Scotland to be shipped to Leith in time to be used for the erection of the Tattoo stands. At the conclusion of the Tattoo, its scaffolding material was distributed to destinations throughout Scotland thus leaving no storage problems between Tattoos.

James Sibbald takes up the story:

> It would seem that the company recognised the publicity value of the high profile the stand construction provided and in consequence offered their services at a very reasonable price, whilst at the same time using photographs of the Tattoo in company advertising material. It therefore came as something of a surprise when we were informed that the price charged did not cover costs, and a more realistic price would be some £40,000 more than the price charged for the previous year.
>
> The Policy Committee instructed the City Architect to look into alternative methods of constructing spectator seating. It so happened, he had recently been impressed by a novel development which had come to his attention with the erection of a kinetic sculpture on a roundabout in Edinburgh's Picardy Place.

The MERO System was a German product. An 'air frame' was created with steel balls of various sizes into which are crossed hollow tubes. The stands were constructed in this manner, and designed using computer technology. Replacement of re-designed spectator boxes erected on top of the East Stand was also required, and as the planning of the new stands progressed, it became clear that further problems required to be overcome. 'The old scaffolding stands had been so erected that downward pressure exerted by the weight of the stands and spectators was distributed along the length of the stands at the numerous points at which the scaffolding tubes rested on the surface of the Esplanade.

The design of the new stands, however, necessitated 'point loading' which meant that the weight of the stands and the spectators would be born at only a few points along the stands' length. Bore holes revealed that the solum of the Esplanade was supported by material imported from Edinburgh's New Town some two hundred years before, from the excavation of buildings there.

This infill material overlay the more steep rock forming the earlier approach to the Castle. It was necessary, therefore, to anchor the new stands to bedrock which lay at various depths up to forty feet below the present surface. Much hectic, dusty drilling work took place in the Spring of 1975 to place these rock anchors, to which were attached concrete pillars rising to the surface upon which the new stands were attached.

Such work greatly increased the total cost of the stands and spectator boxes and Tattoo expenditure over the next ten years had to fund costs of the debt incurred by the City of Edinburgh District Council on behalf of the Tattoo. However, the debt was finally extinguished in 1985.

The new stands with their increased seating capacity soon proved their worth, being very well received, but there was one body of opinion which was not always complimentary about the Tattoo.

16.1 and 16.2 Behind the scenes. (*above left*) The pipers rehearse and (*above*) a dancer from the Central Band of the Russian Navy gets read

Relations with Edinburgh Castle's nearest neighbours, the residents of Ramsay Garden, have over the years ranged between benign acceptance and fierce confrontation. Cecil Stout recorded that on a number of occasions exchanges took place between the Tattoo Policy Committee and the Ramsay Garden Proprietors' Association.

These usually took the form of correspondence between secretaries, and telephone conversations – a memorable one taking place well after midnight on a dress rehearsal night from an irate resident demanding that the Joint-Secretary, asleep in bed when the call came, immediately stop the military band presently playing below the caller's window as the vibration it was giving off was causing his valuable French chandelier to oscillate.

Certainly members of the Policy Committee visited the houses to hear complaints during performances and the proprietors sent delegations to be interviewed by the Policy Committee at the City Chambers. The hostile reaction it appeared centred on three main topics (1) the length of time taken to erect the stands before the Tattoo and to dismantle them afterwards, also the elimination of light from the rooms in houses close to the erected stands; (2) the noise created by the erectors, and (3) the noise of the Tattoo itself and the crowds attending performances.

Then in 1975, the residents of Ramsay Garden found the additional works being carried out on the Esplanade the final straw and James Sibbald firmly believed that it was this that finally propelled the Association into taking the action it took shortly afterwards.

This was the well-publicised case in which a young lady supported by the Residents' Association and financed by legal aid, took the Tattoo to court with the object of having it removed from the Castle Esplanade altogether. Although her action was unsuccessful, the outcome was that the Tattoo was restrained in future from 'causing nuisance by reason of metallic noise in the erection etc, of the spectator stands'.

Thereafter, according to Major Leishman, much merriment was caused by the use of rubber hammers and rubber sheeting. Much of the disturbance, defined on appeal as 'the banging of steel on steel', had been caused by the hammer blows needed to ascertain a correct fit of the giant mechano set that makes up the Tattoo's stands. The fact that the contractor now managed to eliminate the impromptu musical accompaniment of the steel workers whilst waiting for the next piece of stand section was indeed a major factor in reducing the noise levels previously associated with the work. The measurement of sound levels throughout each day of construction now is an ongoing and costly addition to the organisation, and it should no doubt be recorded that whereas the lady's costs after legal aid were negligible, the Tattoo was required to meet substantial expenses.

However, the financial position of the Tattoo was by now secure although the size of surpluses varied year on year. Inflation continued to cause costs to rise, but the arrival of a new source of income greatly assisted in the maintenance of ticket purchase prices at an affordable level. This income came from sponsorship from the private sector.

The Tattoo's first sponsor was the Bank of Scotland, to be followed by Invergordon Distillers, the makers of Glayva, the whisky liqueur.

Meanwhile, the reserve Fund continued to increase with the figure of £200,000 achieved in 1984, and £250,000 by 1986. Annual donations to service charities and the Festival Society were revised in such a way as to secure that after an appropriate slice of any surplus had been placed in reserve, the next £4,000 should go to service charities and the remainder divided equally between service charities and the Festival Society. This arrangement reflected a justifiable advantage to the service charities in that the services' input to the Tattoo was the principal factor in producing surpluses.

Then, in 1987, another financial challenge presented itself. The spectator boxes were now twelve years old, having been designed for a fifteen-year lifespan. Intrinsic faults in design were allowing the ingress of water during bad weather and additionally, the mechanics of fixing the boxes to the structure of the stands was starting to cause concern.

The City Architect, responsible for issuing the public entertainment licence, now annually required by the Tattoo, presented the committee with an ultimatum. This boiled down to two alternatives: 'either replace the boxes or spend at least £80,000 on radical refurbishment of the existing ones'. If the latter course were taken, then the issue of a licence could only be guaranteed for one year.

This in substance was a matter of 'Hobson's Choice' and the Policy Committee decided to have new boxes constructed. Enquiries by the City Architect produced a report indicating that these could be manufactured at an estimated cost of either £250,000 or £350,000 depending upon the chosen design. At the lower figure the Tattoo's reserve fund was just sufficient to meet the cost, although this would leave the coffers bare. However, the Policy Committee favoured the more expensive design and resolved to approach the City of Edinburgh District Council as it had done before in 1974 with the request that the council use its borrowing powers, once again on the basis of reimbursement by the Tattoo.

But things had changed greatly since 1974, and the District Council considered that in view of its own priorities, it would have the greatest difficulties in attempting to include a figure of £250,000 within the allocation for capital projects permitted by the Secretary of State for Scotland in that financial year. The Council therefore told the Policy Committee to see if they could raise the sum of money required elsewhere.

It was at this point that the Council's Director of Administration

16.3 The Pipes and Drums march on to the Esplanade

suggested that if the Tattoo were to become a limited company, there would be no problem with the company entering into a commercial contract to borrow the required amount. A further advantage was that the Tattoo would acquire legal status. The Policy Committee therefore accepted this advice, and consequently, in 1988, The Edinburgh Military Tattoo Ltd was incorporated.

Of course, it had been envisaged that existing members of the Tattoo

147

Policy Committee would automatically form the Board of Directors of the new company, but it turned out that this would be impossible because the Ministry of Defence refused to permit serving officers to assume the responsibilities of a company director. This difficulty was overcome however by the appointment of two senior retired army officers as directors, with the serving officers meeting together as an advisory group to assist the Board in decision making only.

The Lord Provost of Edinburgh was automatically appointed company Chairman and the board was completed by the appointment of one elected member of the District Council, the Director of Finance, the Producer and the Business Manager. The joint secretary appointed by the city to the former Policy Committee simply became Company Secretary.

For many years, Lothian and Borders Fire Brigade has had a close association with the Tattoo. There are some who even remember the Brigade's first performance in 1963, but as was pointed out by Robert S. Virtue, the Brigade's Community Education Officer, they first 'performed' in 1956 when fire broke out in one of the stands during a performance. It was when he observed this display of fire fighting that it occurred to Brigadier Maclean that it might be a good idea to include them at a future date.

Even so, most Tattoo audiences are unaware that whilst they are in the stands and enjoying the spectacle, a fire brigade picket is constantly checking for the risk of fire or hazard. Unseen, a fire crew is always on stand-by. The 'picketing' goes back to the early days of the Tattoo, and a collective sigh of relief was breathed when an access tunnel to the Castle was finally constructed. Gone are the nightmare memories of the previous access only by way of the drawbridge and portcullis entrance.

During the 1950s and 1960s, security mainly involved ensuring that neither audience nor performers had consumed too much alcohol, trying to stop wee boys from sneaking in free, keeping the High Street relatively free from the odd extra car, and the management of the crowds. Sadly, from the early 1970s onwards, a lot of innocence was lost in public life.

16.4 The lone piper – Pipe Major Angus MacDonald

Today safety standards have become a preoccupation with governments and local authorities alike. After tragedies such as the Hillsborough Football Stadium disaster, the Tattoo was ordered to remove ten per cent of its seating, reducing capacity from close on 10,000 to close on 9,000. In addition, a monumental restructuring of stand seating arrangements was required with restrictions on seating and gangways widened to a new standard width.

By the 1990s, security had become big business. For example, provision of twenty-four-hour exit signs resulted in an expensive two-year improvement programme given that the first implementation was considered unsatisfactory.

Each Tattoo season ends with a security co-ordinating conference to discuss lessons learned, and these form the basis of a very comprehensive plan which is then developed over the following 363 or so days. The most frightening and worst case scenarios are considered, and preventative measures swing into operation well before it is time for the stands to be erected again. After that the guard is not lowered until the last performer has departed for home and the Esplanade returned to its normal condition.

# 17   Tattoo International

IN 1976 the organisers of the Edinburgh Military Tattoo became involved with two other Tattoos. The first of these took place in Hobart, Tasmania. At the request of the Tasmanian Authorities, Colonel Sandy Storm, up until 1974 Brigadier Sanderson's Assistant Producer, devised an event based almost entirely upon the Edinburgh concept. In March he put this spectacle on with the assistance of Captain John MacLellan from the Army School of Piping at Edinburgh Castle, Miss Noel Nicol of the Manor School of Dancing in Edinburgh, Colonel Douglas Spratt and Alex Thain.

The Tasmania Tattoo, the first of its kind in the Antipodes, and showing items the majority of which had previously appeared in Edinburgh, was extremely successful. Equally well received was the second Tattoo exported from Edinburgh that year. Sponsored by the Ministry of Defence and produced in Washington, it might more accurately be described as a British tattoo with a strong Scottish bias.

The story of this undertaking began towards the end of 1974 when Mrs Jouett Shouse, an American philanthropist, approached Alex Thain to ask for help in providing a tattoo for the American Bicentennial programme. He referred her to the production office.

First reactions up at the Castle were cautious to say the least. Here were Colonel Dow and Colonel Murray in the midst of producing their first Edinburgh Tattoo for August being asked to set up and present another one some six weeks ahead of it in June. But the opportunity seemed such a special one. It would have been regrettable had Edinburgh turned down the opportunity to play a leading part in what was to become Britain's major offering to Washington's bicentennial celebrations.

Mrs Shouse was insistent that the emphasis of the Washington Tattoo must be Scottish and that is how it was planned, except that there were items in it which were characteristically English, thus retaining a broadly based national bias. However, it nonetheless included the pipes and drums of three Lowland regiments and the regimental military bands of two Highland regiments.

These were preceded by state trumpeters playing an open fanfare and followed by the corps of drums from the battalions of The Royal Regiment of Fusiliers. Next came Scottish Dancing – the Lochaber Broadswords danced by men of The 1st Battalion Queen's Own Highlanders, followed by Sergeant Westhead of the battalion dancing the Sean Truibhas solo.

Ending the first half was a Grand Military Fantasia based on the marches, songs and patriotic tunes which have stirred the hearts of the British and American peoples over two centuries, arranged and conducted by Lieutenant Colonel Trevor Sharpe, director of music at the Royal Military School of Music, Kneller Hall, and senior director of music in the British Army. In his inimitable manner, Tom Fleming provided the commentary.

Buglers from The Royal Green Jackets summoned the audience back to their seats after the interval, and the second half began with an item called The Queen's Guards. A small party from The 2nd Battalion Coldstream Guards, accompanied by Yeoman Gaoler R. Harton from the Tower of London, gave an abridged rendering of the ceremony of the keys.

Pipe Major John Allan, Queen's Own Highlanders, chief instructor at the Army School of Piping at Edinburgh Castle and senior pipe major in the British Army contributed a *Lament for the Children* on pibroch and was followed by the United States Army Chorus singing Scots songs.

Hereafter the Washington Tattoo became a joint offering, effected in Tunes of Glory with the participation of the Presidential Salute Gun Platoon firing blanks at the appropriate moments of Laurie Johnston's *Battle Music*. Then there was Scottish country dancing, two dances named *Sugar Candy* and *The World Turned Upside Down* prepared and danced by cadets from the officers' training corps of the Universities of Aberdeen, Edinburgh and Heriot-Watt, Glasgow and Strathclyde, and Tayforth, accompanied by a ceilidh band drawn from the Scottish Regiments attending the show.

Between the dances Captain Sally Floyd performed a Hebridean dance *Flora Macdonald's Fancy* accompanied by the pipes of the Royal Scots. The dance of *The World Turned Upside Down* was created for the Bicentennial by Miss Noel Nicol. After their surrender at Yorktown in 1781, the British Troops are said to have marched out to the tune featured in this new dance.

The main difference from the Edinburgh Tattoo was that the show was being performed in a theatre with a large stage and first class theatre facilities, but which was also largely open air. The acoustics were superb, and an audience of 3,500 was accommodated behind the theatre on the grass.

Totalling some 320 performers, the Washington entertainment was to date the largest British Army tattoo event to be staged abroad. Given considerable backing by the British Foreign and Commonwealth Office, and by the American Bi-Centennial Arts Commission, it also had support from the US Ministry of Defence. Added to this, the Duke of Edinburgh agreed to become its patron and indeed attended in person, as did President Ford.

After six performances in Washington, the production team was back at work in mid-July for the final run up to that year's Edinburgh Tattoo. It was to be another twenty-four years before they – a producer and his production team – became directly involved in staging a similar overseas event, but in the meantime, the Edinburgh Military Tattoo can be said to have directly influenced the production of tattoos in Durban, South Africa, Copenhagen in Denmark, Brisbane and Sydney in Australia, and Nova Scotia in Canada.

17.1 The full-size replica back-drop of Edinburgh Castle in Wellington, New Zealand

Moreover, in March 2000, the Edinburgh Tattoo producer, production team and 300 musicians were given permission by the Ministry of Defence to fly to Wellington, New Zealand to stage four shows. Musicians from the Royal Marines, The Scots Guards and Highland and Lowland bands took part, and the cast, which also included hundreds of New Zealand army musicians and performers from the South Seas, spent just four days rehearsing before sell-out performances, a major attraction of the New Zealand Arts Festival.

Against a full-sized replica backdrop of Edinburgh Castle in the Westpac Trust Stadium on Wellington's quayside, audiences of 80,000 witnesssed the massed pipes and drums of six Scottish regiments and New Zealand bands marching in formation. The show exploded into life with eight cannons fired from the castle ramparts, featured British army brass bands, New Zealand massed military bands, the Fijian Military Forces Band, spear-wielding warriors, a spine-tingling Maori haka with more than one hundred participants, and Scottish country dancers. The lone piper was Senior Pipe Major Bruce Hitchings, originally from the city of Palmerston North, who performed *My Home*. New Zealand's Governor General, Sir Michael

Hardie Boys, took the opening night salute, and on another night it was taken by Edinburgh's Lord Provost, Eric Milligan.

'I went into this with some fear and trepidation because it was a different arena and we had everything to consider, from the cannon to the lighting,' reflected Brigadier Jameson afterwards.

He need not have worried. As the 300 pipes and drums emerged from the replica drawbridge onto the arena, three times the width of the Esplanade of Edinburgh Castle, a voice from the crowd was overheard to exclaim, 'Awesome'.

17.2 The real thing

# 18   The Sound of Music

MUSICAL preparation for the display of pipes and drums has changed very little over the years, although regimental pipe bands are today fewer in number and the time allocated for the full blown rehearsal prior to the opening night has been dramatically curtailed.

Also, with fewer regiments in the British Army, bands are far more likely to be in demand for operational tours overseas than they were in the past. This, coupled with the Tattoo's needs to keep costs down as much as possible, makes time more precious, a rather different situation from the days when performers arrived in Edinburgh for two

18.1 Trumpeters of The Band of The Royal Marines

weeks of practice. Now they have two days before the first full rehearsal which is performed on a Wednesday morning in front of the General Officer Commanding the Army in Scotland and Edinburgh's Lord Provost.

Today tunes are chosen at various meetings and distributed at least six months in advance to the participating bands wherever they are stationed. The Director of Army Bagpipe Music is ultimately responsible for putting together the pipe music, but at the same time the various pipe majors and drum majors will ensure that their bands learn the tunes and beatings prior to the big day when they all meet up with one another. During this period there are many phone calls between participating bands to ensure everybody is playing the tunes in the same style.

Much of the credit for this must be given to Lieutenant-Colonel David Murray who, although he was head-hunted as assistant producer and commentator in 1975, had a long association with Edinburgh Tattoo performances going back to the very beginning. Born in Pakistan, Murray was educated at George Watson's School in Edinburgh before joining his father's regiment, The Cameronians (Scottish Rifles) at the outbreak of World War Two.

'I never wanted to be typecast as a Tattoo type,' he said. Nevertheless, having served in the Gulf, then the Ministry of Defence, he was providing his considerable expertise as a piper at the first post-war parades. In 1952 he began getting the pipes properly tuned and the tones right to play throughout the performance. 'Back in the beginning, military directors were military directors,' he said. 'Sam Rhodes of The Scots Guards was very much in charge and could spot a wrong note in a band 400 strong. Colonel Pope of The Coldstream Guards was the same.'

When Murray returned in 1975 he found that a great deal of the musical discipline had lapsed so he began to reintroduce it again in earnest which, he said, 'didn't go down too well in some quarters'. Nevertheless, his efforts soon resulted in the Assistant Director of the Berlin Symphony Orchestra telling him one night that in his opinion no orchestra could play such a programme so faultlessly without a conductor.

18.2 The Massed Pipes and Drums in formation

Piping had been David Murray's hobby all his life which enabled him to play and talk to pipe majors on an equal level, an invaluable talent. The musical disciplines and many of the ideas he introduced in his five years as Assistant Director, such as flagpoles and sentries at the castle gates, are maintained to this day. In 1994, he published *Music of The Scottish Regiments*, considered a classic of its kind.

With rehearsals completed, it was straight on with the show, but as the Tattoo grew, so did the outside commitments. Bands are now expected to be available for the Festival Cavalcade on Princes Street, the Glasgow March with display to follow in George Square, and the now traditional contingents parade at Princess Margaret Rose Hospital.

Major Gavin Stoddart, Director of Army Bagpipe Music since 1990, admitted that he has always been amazed at the speed with which the bands pull things together. 'Today, in one and a half days, we have a show. In many ways it is a miracle,' he said.

But the miracle does not come about without months of organisation and long distance commitment beforehand, made even more remarkable by the introduction of participants from other countries, even when they had a week to rehearse.

In 1975, for example, no less than five police bands from Australia took part in the performance, each travelling independently. Special Constable Macgregor Boyd Napier, OAM, first instructor of the Western Australia Police Band, and Special Constable John McMurtrie, gave an illuminating account of just exactly what was involved in bringing over one of these full size bands from the other side of the world.

Twenty-two members took part, with Inspector K.G. Parnell, appointed officer in charge of the Western Australia contingent. Other and larger bands came from Queensland, Victoria, Tasmania and New South Wales, the latter being the largest. 'Our band from Western Australia was the underdog, but in the end we were proud of ourselves,' said Special Constable Napier.

The bandsmen departed from Perth Airport on Friday 11th July, arriving the following day at Heathrow in London from where they were transported via Colchester to Edinburgh by bus. Redford Barracks they found freezing cold in comparison to where they had come from, and they had just made up their beds when a 'squaddie' arrived from the quartermaster to say that the number of each mattress had to be checked, so the beds had to be stripped again. They also had to clean out the ablutions, which were mildewed, to put it politely, as the barracks had not been occupied since the previous battalion had departed for Northern Ireland.

With very little sleep they were awakened the next morning by a deafening fanfare as the trumpeters also stationed in the barracks began rehearsing well before 8am. There followed nine days of their own rehearsal, seven at Redford, then dry runs at the castle. On 21 August the young bandsmen were in full ceremonial uniform and raring to go when a full search of the buses taking the band to the Castle was made for 'explosive devices'. Much to their collective relief none was found.

18.3 'Hear no evil' – the conductor of the Central Band of the Russian Navy during rehearsals

In total, there were twenty bandsmen and two police cadets with the Western Australia Pipe Band, including Ross Napier, who aged seventeen-and-a-half played *Sleep, Dearie, Sleep* before an audience of 9,000 when he was one of the three Australians invited to be the Lone Piper that year.

Bandsmen were paid five pence per performance, but not for rehearsal, and altogether the group received £400. They finished their last performance on Friday 13 September, returning to the barracks at 1am and had to immediately set about packing up their kit to be ready for the buses arriving at 6am to take them to Heathrow. Back in Perth, Western Australia, two days later, a great welcome awaited them, and the video of their visit to the 1975 Tattoo has pride of place in Perth's police library.

Exhausting yet exhilarating, a great international well of cama-raderie was created among the bands who attended the Edinburgh Tattoo over those years.

Major Rodney Parker, invited to be Tattoo Director of Music for

1986, recalled the preparations and administration involved as being the most exciting task of his career.

It started in November 1985. I was in Hong Kong when I received a military telex asking me to take on the job. As Director of Music of the Band of The Brigade of Gurkhas I was based at the Sek Kong depot in the New Territories for a few weeks to produce the Gurkha's annual Sounding Retreat. The telex I received to notify me of my posting to the Tattoo was, as usual, a flimsy six inch square of paper containing a few abbreviated sentences of service jargon, but the beginning of almost a year's work which culminated in the walk down of the final performance – the very last 'Black Bear' of 1986.

On returning to the UK it wasn't too long before I was up in Colonel Leslie Dow's office in Edinburgh Castle for our first meeting. At that stage we discussed the various musical acts which had already been booked for the show and we looked at some ideas for the Finale. The Army in Scotland was well represented with pipes and drums from the Scots Guards, The Black Watch, The Argyll and Sutherland Highlanders and the Edinburgh Boys' Brigade.

Pipes and drums and dancers were also coming from The Argyll and Sutherland Highlanders of Canada, whom I was to meet a year later on their home ground in Hamilton, Ontario. Military bands were booked from The King's Own Scottish Borderers, The Black Watch, The Royal Anglian Regiment, The Gurkhas and, most interestingly, from Germany in the form of Heeresmusikkorps 300 from Koblenz.

Finally we planned the musical content. Bearing in mind the international flavour of this Tattoo and the fact that it was to feature the first public performances given by a German band in the UK in living memory, it was decided to adapt a 'Comrade-in-Arms' approach, peppered with some sing-along favourites and a medley of Scots tunes to round off the display. We therefore entered to the march *Old Comrades*, slow-marched to *Daisy Bell*, gyrated to Sousa's march *Hands Across the Sea*, and came to a halt with the popular theme tune from the TV series *Dallas*.

Having got the audience to warm their hands by clapping along to this we then let them air their tonsils by singing along to a selection of Scottish favourites which I had put together called *Highland Fling*.

The music for an Edinburgh Finale has to provide for four separate sequences: getting everybody on into the form of a spectacular tableau; bringing on the guards of honours in military style; a sequence which takes in the evening hymn, 'Last Post', a lone piper, and 'Auld Lang Syne', and finally, you have to get everybody off!

Then there is an extra feature on Saturday nights which is the firework display over the castle when all the performers are allowed to 'about-turn' and view the spectacle with the audience – a thoughtful touch by the production staff.

Pipe Major Gavin Stoddart, director of Army Bagpipe Music and a member of the Tattoo's production team, was born in Hamburg where his father was serving with the Scottish Airborne Division. The family moved back to Edinburgh in 1948, and Gavin's love of pipe music was fired when his father, Pipe Major George Stoddart of The Royal Scots Fusiliers and Lowland Brigade stationed at Penicuik, was put in charge of the massed pipes and drums and became the Tattoo's first Lone Piper on the castle battlements. Not surprisingly, he can vividly remember attending his first Tattoo in 1954, where his brother David, doing his National Service, was also on parade.

Gavin was performing as a guest piper with the Edinburgh City Police Pipe Band before the age of fifteen, and in 1966 enlisted with The Scots Guards. His initial intention had been to leave after his three year contract was up and join the police force, but he changed his mind. Piping was his great love, and in 1978 he joined the Army School of Piping at Edinburgh Castle as Assistant Director under Pipe Major John Allan. Three years later, on John's retirement, Gavin took over as Director, and when he subsequently became a member of the Tattoo's production and administration team, the school's involvement with the annual event became even more intimate.

18.4 Major Gavin Stoddart, Director of Army Bagpipe Music since 1990, with HRH The Countess of Wessex

Stoddart maintains that up until 1975, despite senior pipe majors being in charge of the musical input, there was no serious organisation of tuning and the setting of the tunes. 'That came when Colonel David Murray took over as assistant producer with special responsibility for pipes and drums, and he began to mould the participants into one complete sound. The quality has been improving ever since.' This despite the Options for Change report of 1991 which led to a number of regiments with pipe bands amalgamating. 'We are still producing more pipe bands than would seem possible and the standards have never been higher,' said Gavin Stoddart with pride.

18.5 The Kevock Choir

In the tradition of the great Jimmy Shand, who composed a tune for the Dundee Military Tattoo during the 1950s, Stoddart in 1996 composed a march called *Edinburgh Military Tattoo*, which is regularly played. For the year 2000, Pipe Major Stuart Samson of the Highlanders, Stoddart's assistant, composed *The Golden Jubilee of the Edinburgh Military Tattoo*.

Another regular and much acclaimed musical input into Tattoo performances since 1982 has been the Kevock Choir, which first collaborated with the Army the year before when it took part in a Royal British Legion (Scotland) Diamond Jubilee Gala Concert in Stirling. Writing in the Kevock Choir newsletter, the founder and conductor

Alex Elrick explained that for the 1982 Edinburgh Military Tattoo, it had been suggested that the finale should be a partially animated 'Son et Lumière' depicting Napoleon's Retreat from Moscow. Some soldiers dressed for the part could fire blanks at each other and Napoleon on his horse could appear from the back-drop of the floodlit Castle with bags of 'Son' and lots of 'Lumière'. Tchaikovsky's *1812 Overture* was the natural choice to go with this, and the gun fire would be for real.

'But there's a choir in the 1812,' somebody had interspersed.

'Oh, is there? Well, let's try the Kevock again. They can sing some Scottish songs as well, and they'll be cheaper than bringing over the North Borneo Mounted Levies Male Voice Choir.' And so the association became established.

'We had to bring a lot of feet firmly back to earth,' said Alex Elrick. 'There were twenty-six performances in three weeks, plus rehearsals each night for a week beforehand. The European and Trans-Atlantic sales of the BBC TV recording were estimated to be seen by 140 million people, so if you picked your nose at the wrong moment an awful lot of people were going to know about it. Statistically, it always rained on about five nights. And each Friday and Saturday would be a double performance.'

Between sixty and seventy choristers were needed each evening. All the members of the Kevock Choir had jobs or lessons to study, not to mention families to bring up. From a choir of 120 members, the conductor had to round up sixty-five individuals, add in some reserves, and still achieve a balance for each performance. Coach and mini-bus trips had to be organised to travel around Dalkeith, Penicuik, Edinburgh and outlying villages to get different choir members to the Castle and home again nightly for a month.

From the start it was agreed with Lieutenant Colonel Dow that the choir would be pre-positioned on a suitably tiered platform erected without too much jeopardy to life and limb or the Health and Safety Act, where it could be floodlit. Public address equipment was hired to put nearly 3,000 watts of choral sound from eight microphones over the extensive Castle ramparts.

The lady choir members kept warm by investing in white wool jumpers to wear about their long tartan skirts under which, according to insider information, they have been known to wear anything from corduroys to sleeping bags. Plastic see-through macs would be used on rainy nights, but the hair and mascara had to look after themselves. The men were grateful to the Lothian and Borders Police Force who loaned them police raincoats to put over their dinner jackets when the 'wet weather' order was given, 'but it was never raining until the army said it was,' added Elrick.

The Kevock Choir began its performance in 1982 with a group of Scottish and military songs arranged by its conductor, largely unaccompanied, but with short, effective introductions to set the key by the band of The Grenadier Guards under that year's musical director Major Derek Kimberley. The problems started at the first rehearsal. Sound travels 1100 feet a second, and the band was one hundred yards away down the Esplanade. If the choir or band began listening to each other, half a second went adrift very rapidly, and the echo did not help.

Major Kimberley did his best, altering the stage management to place his band where the time differential and echo was least intrusive to the choir and least noticeable to the audience. But everything had to be done by sight and sight only. The Kimberley baton followed the Kevock conductor's arms exactly.

On one occasion, however, the choir had just received the expected stirring Grenadier introduction to the song *Johnnie Cope* in G Minor when a speeding fire-engine in Princes Street below repeatedly blared out a sort of F Sharp, E Flat to the choir, the sound flattening as it went by. 'Under the circumstances Cope was extremely fortunate to get his "Challenge from Dunbar" off the ground in anything approaching G Minor,' said Elrick.

The rehearsal for the *1812 Overture* opened with The Grenadier Guards almost under the battlements where the Kevock Choir was positioned, and it was intended that the time should be taken from Major Kimberley direct. Accordingly, the singers launched into 'Spa zee gos po dee' with very few problems until the first 'Kreh Stom', which is half a beat after the bar beat.

All the musicians were properly trained to operate on the bar beat, and Kimberley, concentrating on them, realised just too late that most amateur choristers require a bit of help with off-beat entries, particularly when their Russian is not what it might be.

18.6 The Pipes and Drums lead on to the Esplanade

Said Alex Elrick, 'That incident brought home to us how magnificent the Kimberleys of this world are at coping with ceremonial and the great occasion. On our side, about seventy lots of adrenalin we didn't know we possessed were making it rather difficult to breathe. On his side, a slightly more imperious wave of his non-batoned arm on the half-beat next time round indicated he had spotted our mistake, and understood. When you become flustered, it is always reassuring to know that the man at the helm has not.'

As the *1812* progressed, The Grenadiers were joined by most of the other Scottish bands not on Ireland or Falkland duty, progressing in a slow march to the other end of the Esplanade, some 190 musicians building up the scene in impressive splendour.

Russian shot Frenchman and Frenchman shot Russian. The noise of rattling harness, gun carriages and neighing horses came over the public address system adding realistically to the fog of war. Tchaikovsky would have been impressed, wrote a choir member. 'Particularly when the equivalent of Mons Meg went off on the battlements just behind us. Half the sopranos all but jumped into the castle moat, but that's what rehearsals are for, and we quickly became adequately if not completely battle-seasoned!'

'Come the second 'Spa zee gos po dee', Major Kimberley was a small, impressive floodlit speck in the distance whose arms we all watched as though our lives depended upon them, climaxing in 'God the Omnipotent' with a sigh of relief that their battle – and ours – was about over.'

The Evening Hymn was an arrangement by David Kimberley of 'Crimond' and the 'Last Post', which everybody found to be deeply moving. On one evening's south-easterly breeze, three kilowatts of Kevock were wafted clearly to Calton Hill, a mile away over Waverley Station and Princes Street, and the following day the conductor received a call from an unknown spectator to be informed that the choir's 'Crimond' had brought tears to the eyes. 'I know,' he replied, unmoved. 'In my case, as their conductor, I find that this is a not infrequent occurrence.'

18.7 The Massed Bands

# 19   A Lifetime of Spectacle

AFTER fifteen years, Lieutenant-Colonel Leslie Dow bade farewell to his beloved Edinburgh Military Tattoo, giving failing health as his reason for leaving. In retirement he fully intended to embark upon writing a full history of the Tattoo, and indeed began the research which has made this book possible by sending out questionnaires to past participants. Sadly he died in January 1991, just before he could get properly started.

In the meantime, Major Michael Parker, who succeeded him as Producer for a period of three years, introduced a dramatically more flamboyant and themed style of Tattoo, influenced by the remarkable variety of Army spectacles he had orchestrated elsewhere. Michael Parker claimed to have produced his first Army tattoo in 1965, almost by accident, when as a second lieutenant in the Queen's Own Hussars he apparently impressed the top brass so much with his organisational skills at regimental dances that they asked him to organise a show. When he protested his youth and inexperience to his commanding officer, he was told simply to get on with it. 'The commanding officer told me that as a mere second lieutenant I had nothing to lose!' he said.

Educated at Dulwich College and Hereford Cathedral School, Parker attended the Royal Military Academy Sandhurst before joining The Queen's Own Hussars in 1961. After first producing the Berlin Tattoo in 1965, he was to go on to produce military spectacles the world over, including the British Festival in Berlin for twenty years, and the Royal Tournament in London until 1999.

In 1981 he was responsible for staging the musical fireworks for the

19.1  Major Michael Parker

wedding of the Prince and Princess of Wales, and in 1990 he put together the national tribute to mark the ninetieth birthday of HM Queen Elizabeth the Queen Mother on London's Horse Guard's Parade. The following year he mounted a grand spectacle at Buckingham Palace as the finale to the group of Seven Nation's 'G7' economic summit, and in 1992 produced both the British National Day at Expo '92 in Seville and the important autumn celebrations to commemorate the fortieth anniversary of the accession to the throne of HM Queen Elizabeth.

It was a busy year, but despite his other commitments, he was a natural to take on the challenge of Edinburgh, and he immediately brought a more theatrical input into the spectacle, providing story-lines for each show and heightening the spectacle.

'Michael prepared scripts as to what might make a show,' said Alasdair Hutton, broadcaster, journalist and a former Member of the European Parliament, who became the Edinburgh Tattoo's narrator in 1992. 'He introduced little dramatic tables with thespians and dramatic light and had a wonderful predilection for fire and introduced the big braziers and torches at the Castle gates. In 1993 we even had a burning Viking longboat.'

From the start, Parker co-opted the Scottish Community Drama Association, founded in 1926, to portray Macbeth, witches, and Highland chiefs. He paid tributes to Mary Queen of Scots and King James VI, and a final tableau presented King George IV's visit to Edinburgh in 1822 when the Honours of Scotland, the Crown, the Sword of State and Mace, hidden and forgotten within the Castle walls for a hundred years, were brought forth onto the Esplanade to be presented to him.

Following on this, the 1994 Tattoo paid tribute to the Gordon Highlanders, raised in 1794 by the Duke of Gordon to boost the ranks of the British Army in the war against France, and which was to be disbanded in 1995. The Duke's wife, the Duchess Jean, played a prominent part in the subsequent recruiting, riding to country fairs in Highland bonnet and jacket and giving a kiss to the men she enlisted.

Sometimes, it was said, she placed a shilling between her lips. At one village there was a young blacksmith whom recruiters from the Guards had tried to enlist but in vain. However, he could not resist the Duchess and took the kiss and the shilling, but to show that it was not the money that had won him over, he tossed the shilling to the watching crowd.

Other features in Parker's programmes included a dramatic re-enactment of the Duchess of Richmond's Ball held on the eve of the Battle of Waterloo, the Charge of the Greys and the Gordons, and Ensign Ewart's capture of the French Eagle. Men from the 1st Battalion, The Gordon Highlanders celebrated the five hundredth anniversary of the first mention of Scotch whisky in written text, and the climax of the night came when the massed pipes and drums joined the remainder of the cast in a *Farewell to the Gordons*.

Alasdair Hutton remembered the whisky celebration all too well. 'I had started the introduction and suddenly realised that something was wrong. No leader of the wild Highlanders, so I had to quickly jump to the middle of the script. It later transpired that the gentleman in question had been chatting up one of the young dancers and completely missed his cue.'

19.2 A celebration of the 500th anniversary of the first mention of Scotch whisky distillation in written text

Hutton's enduring reputation as Tattoo commentator was sealed when he unwittingly became a marriage broker. 'Every year at least one person asks me to propose marriage on their behalf,' he said. 'It began with notes from pipers and drummers wanting me to send messages to their grannies and mothers, then one night one of the pipers requested I read out a proposal of marriage for him. That started it. It is very difficult for a girl to say no when she is under a spotlight and everybody is watching.'

Warming up the audience by getting them to sing *Happy Birthday* to somebody was yet another old trick of the trade, as was joining in with the singing, badly. 'It encourages everybody to sing louder,' he explained.

But it has been Alasdair's ending quotation taken from Sir Walter Scott's immortal *Lay of The Last Minstrel* which resounds in the minds of audiences for weeks and months and years thereafter:

> Breathes there the man with soul so dead,
> Who never to himself hath said,
> This is my own, my native land!
> Scotland. Scotland the Brave!

There then follows the traditional 'Scott-Barrett Rocket', named after the former GOC, Sir David Scott-Barrett, who during his tenure as Governor of Edinburgh Castle had always insisted that the Tattoo should end with a bang!

For many years the dates of the Edinburgh Military Tattoo mirrored those of the Edinburgh International Festival and this meant that performances took place each year well into September when the weather in Scotland traditionally breaks to become wet and cold. Nevertheless, when Major Brian Leishman suggested that the Tattoo should get away from this by moving the event to one week earlier, there was considerable opposition.

19.3 and 19.4 (*above left*) A Highland clansman stands guard. (*above*) Rehearsals at Redford Barracks

After much debate, however, the move was agreed, and with due notice the dates were changed. With the Edinburgh International Festival then deciding to follow suit almost immediately, a separation did not materialise. But in 1988 it was still apparent that attendances were falling away in the third week, which still fell in the early part of September and followed the English Bank Holiday weekend. As a result, Leishman was able to convince his fellow board members that they should move back yet another week so that the event would finish on the bank Holiday weekend. Since that move, attendance has increased every year with the result that one hundred per cent capacity audiences are now being achieved.

It is also interesting to reflect that as many as twenty-nine performances were being run at one stage, although happily this was not pursued on the grounds that it was possible to prove that total audiences were pretty constant in the order of 200,000 give or take a few thousand. Whilst a small audience was not necessarily bad, performances should always have as near to full capacity as possible for both psychological reasons and to ensure that the trade does not question the need to book and pay early in the year as opposed to later.

19.5 The Drummers' Salute from
The Royal Marines

A case in point was illustrated by the double Friday performances where the second house audiences were in the order of forty per cent capacity. Good income, poor psychology. After much effort, Leishman was able to persuade his colleagues that it would be better, for a variety of reasons, to move one performance to the Thursday evening which until then had been a free evening. The quid pro quo for this was the elimination of the daytime matinee performance held on one Saturday afternoon during the season.

Another interesting in-house battle was the suggestion that instead of the Tattoo carrying out its own parade along Princes Street on a Monday when there was precious little audience, it should join the *Edinburgh Evening News* Festival Cavalcade on the preceding Sunday, a decision ultimately welcomed by both police and the newspaper. That this victory was followed by Leishman's proposal that the Tattoo should march through Scotland's other great city, Glasgow, was another positive marketing venture.

Awarded the Scottish Silver Thistle Award for services to Scottish tourism in 1996, Major Brian Leishman was the longest serving member of the Tattoo team to date, helping to transform it from, in

19.6 The Gurkhas take part in the *Edinburgh Evening News* Festival Cavalcade

his own words, 'a cosy, comfortable cottage industry' to an event which annually contributes in excess of £40million to the Scottish economy. There followed a Lifetime Achievement Award from New York-based Box Office Management International, recognising his remarkable input into the industry.

Always impeccably dressed, in tartan trews, blazer or dinner jacket, his large gentlemanly presence and booming voice, coupled with a mischievous sense of humour, have played a uniquely significant role in promoting the Tattoo, and Scotland, worldwide, often in as many as ten destinations in ten days.

His philosophy on why it should have such universal appeal is straightforward. 'You don't have to be an enthusiast about the military to enjoy the show, All you have to do is like music and pomp and ceremony. When I see people coming out at the end they are walking as if they are six inches taller – and they have a smile on their face. Yes, it is PR for the Army. But is also show business on a grand scale.'

In 1998, after twenty years as Business Manager, Leishman retired, but continued an involvement with the Tattoo team when he was asked to organise the *Edinburgh Evening News* Festival Cavalcade. As a former Chairman of the Edinburgh Jazz Festival, and board member of Edinburgh and The Lothians Tourist Board, his expertise on the twin demands of administration and entertainment was hard to surpass.

Standing six feet five inches tall, the Major witnessed every twenty-five-night performance over two decades, but has no hesitation in choosing his most emotional moment. It came at a staff Christmas party at which one of the guests was Gavin Stoddart. 'At one point Gavin stood up, rang a bell and announced he had a tune he'd like to play,' said Leishman. 'It was a real tear jerker.'

The tune was a Strathspey entitled *Major Brian A.S. Leishman*, and it was played at the Tattoo on his departure, a fitting tribute to the man who beat the drum so effectively around the world on so many levels for both this historic pageant and for his homeland.

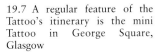
19.7 A regular feature of the Tattoo's itinerary is the mini Tattoo in George Square, Glasgow

# 20 The Millennium

BRIGADIER Melville Jameson had been Commander, 51st Highland Brigade in Perth for only a year when he was summoned in late 1994 to a meeting with General Mike Scott, the General Officer Commanding the Army in Scotland and Governor of Edinburgh Castle.

'I thought he just wanted to ask me how things were going in the Highland Brigade,' he recalled. 'Instead, he asked me if I would be prepared to produce the Tattoo when Mike Parker departed after the 1994 run.'

'I'm sure you'll be able to manage the Highland Brigade as well,' said the General.

And thus the Brigadier embarked upon what he insists has been the most exciting challenge of his life. Not only did he take on the job of Producer, but, later, that of Chief Executive as well. 'With 8,600 people coming through the door on a Thursday and you only get the troops on the Monday before, it can be somewhat daunting,' he admitted.

Melville Jameson was born and brought up at his family home near Blairgowrie in Perthshire and educated at Trinity College, Glenalmond. From the Royal Military Academy of Sandhurst he was commissioned into The Royal Scots Greys, and served in Northern Ireland, Germany, Cyprus, the Middle East, and Edinburgh where, in 1971, the regiment amalgamated with 3rd Caribiniers to form The Royal Scots Dragoon Guards.

Regimental service thereafter included three years as a squadron leader in Chieftain tanks, two years as second in command, and follow-

20.1 Brigadier Melville Jameson

ing a tour as chief of staff, 52 Lowland Brigade based at Edinburgh Castle. In 1986, Jameson was appointed to command The Royal Scots Dragoon Guards from 1986 at Tidworth in Hampshire. Two years later he was posted as directing staff to the Joint Service Defence College, then appointed colonel on the Military Secretary's staff. Following his command of 51 Highland Brigade, he decided to take early retirement in order to concentrate on the Tattoo in December 1996.

Brigadier Jameson's first show, inevitably influenced by his predecessor Michael Parker, celebrated both Scotland's Auld Alliance with France and the two hundred and fiftieth anniversary of the Jacobite Rising. Scottish Country and Highland dancers drawn from the Tattoo Dance Company re-enacted the ball held at Holyrood Palace to honour Bonnie Prince Charlie and his triumphant entry into the city of Edinburgh in front of his Highland army.

Jameson vividly remembers his first rehearsal on a Monday being somewhat chaotic – everyone was depressed at the midnight production meeting except BBC Producer, Justin Adams, who piped up, 'Mel you've got a great show here!' The next day, however, with a cast of 800 soldiers, horses and children, it all came together by a breathtaking miracle. He said, 'Such miracles are often achieved by my excellent Production Manager Steve Walsh, MBE, Ex-Gordons.'

Already the musicality which is Jameson's trade mark was beginning to reveal itself. In 1997 tribute was paid to the Golden Wedding Anniversary of The Queen and Prince Philip. The Trinidad and Tobago Defence Force Steel Band and Drums played Caribbean calypsos. In 1998 the Emerald Isle Irish Dance Team joined the Tattoo's Ceilidh Dancers. The Meke Dancers accompanied the Republic of Fiji Military Forces Band.

And in 1998 for the first time there were Russian performers, the Central Band of the Russian Navy which, although formed as recently as 1941, carried a legacy dating back to the seventeenth century and the reign of Tsar Peter the Great.

With more Caribbean music from the Barbados Defence Force Band and transatlantic rhythm from the Golden Eagles, South East

20.2 The Central Band of the Russian Navy at the unveiling in 1998 of a memorial to Samuel Greig, a native of Inverkeithing and Admiral of Russia

Missouri State University's Marching Band, in 1999, nobody could accuse the Edinburgh Tattoo of being predictable.

Jameson has taken stock of this. 'Statistically, the audience is about twenty-five per cent Scots. There is always a huge English contingent and an ever increasing demand from the USA, Commonwealth and Europe.'

He sees the Tattoo as being supported by a series of pillars to create a strong foundation, indeed a 'traditional recipe'. The most important pillar is the massed pipes and drums and he has increased the number of bands to enhance the sound and spectacle – the Lone Piper is also vital. 'The Lone Piper at the 1950 Tattoo and for eleven years was Pipe Major George Stoddart and in tribute to him, half a century on, his son Major Gavin Stoddart, Director of Army Bagpipe Music, performed as Lone Piper at the 1999 Tattoo.'

Jameson's second pillar is the massed military bands, and the third, 'variety and spice from abroad'. 'Of course, overseas visitors are keen to see the Scottish Acts and the Castle,' he conceded. 'But it is a vital ingredient for the local audience.' He admits that he likes his shows to be predominantly musical.

20.3 Brigadier Melville Jameson introduces HRH The Earl of Wessex to members of the cast

20.4 Fifty years on ... The Trinidad and Tobago Defence Force

20.5 Zulu dancers from South Africa

20.6 The Callisthenic Dancers from South Australia Police

20.7 The Golden Eagles – South East Missouri State University Marching Band

20.8 The Finale, 2000

And the fourth pillar is the Finale, when pipes come together with military bands, choir, fiddles and even electronics, with old favourites such as *Amazing Grace* and *Highland Cathedral* and new arrangements, *Gael, Hector the Hero* and *Land of Light*.

However, he still intends to include action items, particularly for the young members of the audience, spectacles such as Royal Marine Commandos, motorcycle display teams, drill displays and regimental pageants.

To commemorate the fiftieth anniversary of the Tattoo, Brigadier Jameson commissioned a Jubilee tartan, designed by tartan scholar Lieutenant-Colonel Peter MacDonald, incorporating colours from all the Scottish regiments and the city of Edinburgh cloths. 'We used the old dyes and included red from the old band tartan and black for the city of Edinburgh.'

Working up to four years ahead, he has overseas acts booked well in advance as mostly they need to have time to find sponsorship to enable them to come. The Millennium Tattoo was a celebration of the Commonwealth and he was proud to include a large number of acts from the Commonwealth.

'So many Commonwealth countries have regiments with pipes and drums affiliated with Scottish regiments,' he said. 'The entire programme, the music and narration was devised to pay homage to our associations over the years.'

Jameson understands that success does not come easily – he emphasises the importance of 'team work' and he is grateful to his excellent office staff and to his production team – 'They deserve the credit for our recent successes'.

'I have inherited as Chief Executive and Producer a world beater thanks to all my predecessors,' said Jameson. 'It is my responsibility and privilege to guard this legacy and ensure that it goes from strength to strength for the next fifty years.'

# The Lone Piper

Alone ye stand, on the castle's Half Moon,
A wonderous view o' Edinburgh Toon,
From far below, ye hear the crowd,
The singing, echoing clear and loud.

They've seen the acts, o'military precision,
The growing applause is their decision.
But wait. What's this I see approach?

The Esplanade is out of sight.
I canna even see a light.
The mist has covered one and all,
And even the Guard Commander's call.

The Evening Hymn and the Last Post,
Is usually heard from coast to coast.
But, alas, this time I fear
It's something I just couldn't hear.

But still, you always find the cue
From the speaker, concealed by the side of you.
This time . . . of all, you find it's broken
And for your tune no word is spoken.

Yet softly appears the Castle Ghost,
Who really . . . IS the Tattoo host.
He whispers loudly in both ears.
That brings relief, and almost tears.
'Play now, play NOW! This is your cue.
Lights Out. The Tune is Donald Blue.'

So up ye strike and play Lament,
And Ghostie sighs with great content,
'I hope tomorrow there's nae gloom,
I haunt the Officer's Dining Room.'

At last, at last, when I am finished,
The lights have one and all diminished.
Applause. Applause, that's oh so near,
I see the clapping crowds so clear.

The rocket fires, and bursts aglow,
The orders again begin to flow.
The cast march off with great delight,
Leaving only me in sight.

But . . . not so lonely, in whole truth,
There's always Wallace, here wi Bruce.

Pipe Major Allan T. Dippie, BEM.
(Who played at the Edinburgh Tattoo in the years between 1965 and
1990)

# Appendix

## OVERSEAS PARTICIPANTS

| YEAR | PARTICIPANT | COUNTRY OF ORIGIN | TYPE OF EVENT |
|------|-------------|-------------------|---------------|
| 1952 | Netherlands Royal Military Band | Netherlands | Military Band |
| 1952 | 1st Canadian Highland Pipe Band | Canada | Pipe Band |
| 1952 | La Garde Republicaine à Cheval | France | Mounted Band |
| 1955 | Black Watch of Canada Pipe Band | Canada | Pipe Band |
| 1955 | 8th Punjab Regiment Pipe Band | India | Pipe Band |
| 1955 | Kimberley Regiment of South Africa Pipe Band | South Africa | Pipe Band |
| 1955 | Cameron Highlanders from Western Australia Pipe Band | Western Australia | Pipe Band |
| 1955 | Witwatersrand Rifles Pipe Band | South Africa | Pipe Band |
| 1956 | Malay Police Band | Malaysia | Pipe Band & Military Band |
| 1957 | The King's African Rifles | Kenya | Dancing Display |
| 1957 | The Royal Canadian Mounted Police | Canada | Mounted Band |
| 1957 | The Corps of Janissaries – Turkish Army | Turkey | Military Band |
| 1957 | The Royal Danish Life Guard | Denmark | Mounted Band |
| 1958 | US Marine Corps Band, Drums and Bugles Display Team | USA | Display Team |
| 1959 | The 7th Spahis | Algeria/France | Mounted Band |
| 1959 | The Canadian Guards | Canada | Pipes and Drums |
| 1960 | The Greek Royal Guard | Greece | Drill & Dancing Display |
| 1960 | The Lorne Scots, Canada | Canada | Pipe Band |
| 1961 | HM Kongens Garde | Norway | Drill Team & Military Band |
| 1961 | Royal Canadian Engineers | Canada | Display Team |
| 1962 | 61st Cavalry Regiment | India | Mounted Band |
| 1962 | The Sikh Regiment | India | Military Band |
| 1962 | Queen's Own Rifles | Canada | Fanfare Trumpeters |
| 1962 | Black Watch | Canada | Pipe Band |
| 1963 | The Royal Jordan Arab Army | Jordan | Pipe Band & Military Band |
| 1964 | The Bagad of Lann-bihoue - Brittany | France | Pipe Band |
| 1964 | The Barbados Police Band | Barbados | Police Force Band and Dancers |
| 1964 | British Columbia Highland Dancers | Canada | Dancers |
| 1965 | Fiji Military Band | Fiji | Military Band |
| 1966 | The Pakistan Constabulary | Pakistan | Pipes & Drums, Drill & Dance |
| 1967 | The Bersaglieri – Italy | Italy | Military Band & Display Team |
| 1967 | The Jamaica Regiment | Jamaica | Military Band |
| 1968 | The Queen's Guard Rutgers University | USA | Drill Team |
| 1969 | The Royal Danish Life Guards | Denmark | Drill Team & Drum & Fife Band |
| 1969 | The British Columbia Beefeater Band | Canada | Military Band |
| 1970 | The Royal Brunei Malay Regiment | Brunei | Military Band & Display Team |

| YEAR | PARTICIPANT | COUNTRY OF ORIGIN | TYPE OF EVENT |
|------|-------------|-------------------|---------------|
| 1972 | The Singapore Armed Forces | Singapore | Lion Dance, Sword Display & Frog Dance |
| 1972 | HM Kongens Garde | Norway | Military Band & Drill Team |
| 1973 | The Queen's Guard Rutgers University | USA | Drill Team |
| 1974 | Pipes & Drums The Black Watch of Canada | Canada | Pipes & Drums |
| 1974 | Pipes & Drums The Cameron Highlanders of Ottawa | Canada | Pipes & Drums |
| 1974 | The Argyll & Sutherland Highlanders of Canada (Princess Louise's) | Canada | Pipes & Drums |
| 1974 | The Toronto Scottish Regiment | Canada | Pipes & Drums |
| 1974 | The Sri Lanka Police Reserve Hewisi Band | Sri Lanka | Drumming & Dancing with Police Band |
| 1975 | The Royal New Zealand Infantry Regiment | New Zealand | Maori Music & Dancing |
| 1975 | The British Columbia Beefeater Band | Canada | Military Band & Marching Display |
| 1975 | The Pipe Bands of the Australia State Police Forces | Australia | Pipes & Drums |
| 1976 | The Band of the Corps of Carabinieri | Italy | Military Band |
| 1976 | The Berlin Brigade Drill Team | USA | Drill Team |
| 1977 | La Batterie-Fanfare de la Garde Republicaine de Paris | France | Military Band |
| 1978 | Lochiel Marching Team from Wellington | New Zealand | Marching Team |
| 1978 | Royal Hong Kong Police | Hong Kong | Pipes & Drums and Military Band |
| 1979 | Feldmoching Band with Costume Group | Germany | Music & Dancing |
| 1979 | Riadastoana – Kirchheim-Foldkirchen Band with Costume Group 'Isargau' | Germany | Music & Dancing |
| 1980 | The Vancouver Police Band | Canada | Pipes & Drums |
| 1980 | The Queen's Guard Rutgers University | USA | Drill Team |
| 1980 | The Big Brown Music Machine | USA | Military Band |
| 1980 | The City of Wellington Pipe Band | New Zealand | Pipes & Drums |
| 1980 | The Royal Band of HM The Sultan of Oman | Oman | Military Band |
| 1981 | The Canadian Forces Composite Pipe Band | Canada | Pipes & Drums |
| 1981 | Canadiana Dancers | Canada | Dancers |
| 1982 | HM Kongens Garde | Norway | Military Band & Drill Team |
| 1982 | Fanfara dei Bersaglieri | Italy | Musical Display |
| 1983 | Lochiel Marching Team from Wellington | New Zealand | Marching Team |
| 1984 | The Royal Band of HM The Sultan of Oman | Oman | Military Band and Dancers |
| 1984 | The Flagwavers of Florence | Italy | Flagwavers |
| 1984 | Tasmania Police Pipe Band | Australia | Pipes & Drums |
| 1985 | The Royal Hong Kong Police Bands | Hong Kong | Pipes & Drums & Military Bands |
| 1985 | The Queen's Guard Rutgers University | USA | Drill Team |
| 1986 | Heeresmusikkorps 300 | Germany | Military Band |
| 1986 | Argyll & Sutherland Highlanders of Canada (Princess Louise's) from Hamilton, Ontario | Canada | Pipes & Drums |
| 1986 | Canadiana Dancers from Ottawa & Hamilton | Canada | Dancers |
| 1987 | HM Kongens Garde | Norway | Military Band and Drill Team |
| 1987 | The City of Wellington Pipe Band | New Zealand | Pipes & Drums |
| 1987 | Western United States Collegiate Band | USA | Military Band |
| 1987 | Canadian Cadet Pipes & Drums | Canada | Pipes & Drums |
| 1988 | Tobruk Memorial Pipes & Drums | Australia | Pipes & Drums |
| 1988 | Colonial Dancers | Australia | Dancers |
| 1988 | The Hungarian People's Army Ensemble | Hungary | Dancers, etc. |
| 1988 | The Seaforth Highlanders of Canada Association | Canada | Pipes & Drums |
| 1989 | Canadian Cadet Pipes & Drums | Canada | Pipes & Drums |

| YEAR | PARTICIPANT | COUNTRY OF ORIGIN | TYPE OF EVENT |
|---|---|---|---|
| 1990 | South Australian Police Band | Australia | Military Band |
| 1990 | South Australian Drill Team | Australia | Drill Team |
| 1990 | The Quantico Marine Band of the US Marine Corps | USA | Military Band |
| 1991 | The Citadel Band & Pipes of the Military College of South Carolina | USA | Military Band |
| 1991 | Republic of Singapore Police Band | Singapore | Military Band & Pipes & Drums |
| 1991 | Gurkha Contingent Singapore Police Pipes & Drums | Singapore | Pipes & Drums |
| 1991 | Singapore Women Police Pipes & Drums | Singapore | Pipes & Drums |
| 1991 | Singapore Girl Pipers | Singapore | Pipes & Drums |
| 1991 | Kampong Glam Community Centre Lion Dancers of the People's Association of the Republic of Singapore | Singapore | Dancers |
| 1992 | The Mehter Band | Turkey | Military Band |
| 1992 | Adelaide University | Australia | Pipes & Drums |
| 1993 | HM Kongens Garde | Norway | Military Band & Drill Team |
| 1993 | Lochiel Marching Team | New Zealand | Marching Drill |
| 1993 | Wanganui Brass | New Zealand | Military Band |
| 1994 | Rats of Tobruk Pipes & Drums | Australia | Pipes & Drums |
| 1994 | Delta Police Pipe Band (Delta, BC) | Canada | Pipes & Drums |
| 1995 | The Egyptian Musical Group from Cairo | Egypt | Military Band and Pipes & Drums |
| 1995 | La Musique Du 42ème Regiment De Transmissions | France | Military Band |
| 1995 | The Witwatersrand Rifles Pipes & Drums | South Africa | Pipes & Drums |
| 1996 | 2nd Bn The Royal Canadian Regiment | Canada | Pipes & Drums |
| 1996 | The Royal Hong Kong Police | Hong Kong | Pipes & Drums |
| 1996 | The United States Army Band 'Pershing's Own' | USA | Regimental Band |
| 1996 | South Africa Police Service | South Africa | Zulu Dancers |
| 1996 | The United States Army Drill Team | USA | Drill Team |
| 1997 | The Rats of Tobruk Memorial Pipes & Drums | Australia | Pipes & Drums |
| 1997 | Western Australia Police Pipes & Drums | Australia | Pipes & Drums |
| 1997 | 8th Azad Kashmir Regiment (Pasban) | Pakistan | Pipes & Drums |
| 1997 | The Khyber Rifles | Pakistan | Khattak Dancers |
| 1997 | The Lochiel Champion Drill Team | New Zealand | Marching Drill Team |
| 1997 | Trinidad & Tobago Defence Force | Trinidad & Tobago | Steel Band |
| 1998 | The Central Band of the Russian Navy | Russia | Navy Band & Dancers |
| 1998 | Republic of Fiji Military Forces Band & Meke Dancers | Republic of Fiji | Military Band and Meke Dancers |
| 1998 | City of Invercargill Caledonian Pipe Band | New Zealand | Pipe Band |
| 1998 | City of Dunedin Pipe Band | New Zealand | Pipe Band |
| 1999 | Barbados Defence Force | Barbados | Barbados Defence Force Band |
| 1999 | The Golden Eagles | USA | SE Missouri State University Marching Band |
| 1999 | The Vancouver Police Pipe Band | Canada | Pipe Band |
| 2000 | The Black Watch (Royal Highland Regiment) of Canada | Canada | Pipe Band |
| 2000 | The Cameron Highlanders of Ottawa | Canada | Pipe Band |
| 2000 | 5th/6th Battalion The Royal Victoria Regiment | Australia | Pipe Band |
| 2000 | The Cape Town Highlanders | South Africa | Pipe Band |
| 2000 | The Argyll & Sutherland Highlanders of Canada (Princess Louise's) | Canada | Pipe Band |
| 2000 | The Calgary Highlands | Canada | Pipe Band |
| 2000 | The Wellington, West Coast & Taranaki Regiment | New Zealand | Pipe Band |
| 2000 | Ngati Rangiwewehi Maori Group from Rotorua | New Zealand | Maori Dancing and Singing |
| 2000 | The Royal Canadian Mounted Police | Canada | Drill Display |
| 2000 | 121 South Battalion South African Infantry Zulu Dance Team | South Africa | Ceremonial Dancing and Singing |
| 2000 | Band of the South Australia Police | Australia | Police Band |
| 2000 | South Australia Callisthenic Precision Team | Australia | March and Dance Team |
| 2000 | Anarungga Aboriginal Dance Company | Australia | Traditional Dancing |
| 2000 | Trinidad & Tobago Defence Force Steel Orchestra | Trinidad & Tobago | Steel Band |

*Note*: The Appendix only includes participants from overseas. There have, of course, been countless Bands and Acts from the United Kingdom, and the three Services (the Royal Navy, the Army, including the Gurkhas, and the Royal Air Force) who have taken part in the Tattoo over the years, many of whom are mentioned in the text.

# Index